PARISH LITURGY:
A HANDBOOK FOR
RENEWAL

Robert D. Duggan

A **CHURCH** Book
from the National Pastoral Life Center
New York, NY

Library of Congress Cataloguing-in-Publication Data
Duggan, Robert D.
    Parish liturgy: a handbook for renewal / Robert D. Duggan
    p.   cm.
    ISBN: 1-55612-909-2
    1. Catholic Church—Liturgy.   I. Title
    BX1970.D76   1996
    264'.02'001—dc20   96-17943
                                              CIP

Published by the National Pastoral Life Center
18 Bleecker Street
New York, NY 10012-2404

To order, call: 212-431-7825; fax: 212-274-9786; email: nplc@nplc.org

Cover design by Emil Antonucci
(originally published by Sheed & Ward)

CONTENTS

I.

Introduction

The material in this book was written over a period of ten years. The articles were originally composed for *Church Magazine*, a professional journal focused on parish life, where they appeared in "Liturgy Checklist," a regular column aimed at parish liturgy teams. As such, this material has all of the strengths and limitations of its paternity: There is a sense of immediacy to much of the writing, emerging as it did from the author's wrestling with real-life problems of liturgical renewal in a large suburban parish. But there are limitations as well: Reviewing an entire collection of articles spanning a decade also reminded the author how substantial are the constraints when one covers topics of great complexity in a popular column aimed at offering practical advice.

The intended audience is both parish staff and laity who serve on liturgy teams or committees. Little is presumed by way of technical background in liturgical studies. What is presumed is that the readership has a passion for improving the life of prayer at the local level of the parish and a commitment to the hard work that genuine renewal requires. The author's biases will be evident: A conviction that the mandate for liturgical renewal given at the Second Vatican Council was truly the work of the Holy Spirit and that ours is a privileged generation entrusted with the task of beginning that renewal.

History has shown that great renewal movements are fragile things, inevitably meeting with resistance both within the Church and from outside forces. History has also shown how crucial are the first generations of the reform, since in large measure their courage and perseverance determine the direction and depth that the reform will take. We know, sadly, that reform movements in the Church have on occasion been aborted and the needs they were meant to address sometimes went unmet for centuries. The consequences of such missed opportunities have more than once been disastrous.

Our generation is in the midst of a critical period in which the forces of resistance to liturgical renewal appear in the ascendancy. We seem to be in danger of losing sight of the fundamental conviction of the Vatican Council that the Church's life of prayer and worship is in need of reform and renewal. Those who wish to retreat to "the way things were" before the Council—either out of nostalgia or fear of the unknown future—have found sympathetic allies both at the grass roots and at the highest levels of the ecclesiastical bureaucracy.

The work of renewal is always uncertain; and, it is always hard work! The author writes out of the conviction that what happens at the parish level in the next few generations will ultimately determine the future of liturgical renewal. Rome has done its work in the guiding principles contained in *The Constitution on the Sacred Liturgy* and in the reform documents published to date. Now, at the most basic level of Church, we must breathe life into those documents so that true reform and renewal will be a lived experience on the part of God's people.

The essays contained in this collection are often mundane and basic, because the ideas they present are so foundational. But, where else are we to begin? The book is best read in little chunks, as it was written, rather than all at once. Each piece deserves some thought about how it can be translated into practical strategies for change "back home" in your own parish. If you are tempted to say "it can never happen," please remember that virtually everything in this volume came out of what the author was dealing with in his own parish at the time it was written. Not everything has worked just the way it was described in the ideal. But, at least we have been striving for that ideal in committed and persevering fashion.

Liturgy truly is the "work of the people," and whatever of lasting value is contained in this book is owed in large measure to the faith community of which I have been a part during its composition. The people of St. Rose of Lima Parish have been both challenging and comforting to this liturgist-pastor. Their vibrant faith has humbled me; their many talents have left me in awe; their instinctive linkage of liturgy and action for justice has instructed me; their probing questions have challenged me; and, their love has nourished and sustained me. The parish Vision Statement has been and continues to be for me the essence of what this community is about:

"We Are Bread for One Another: Broken . . . We Gather, Nourished . . . We Reach Out." It is to the people of St. Rose of Lima Parish that I dedicate this book, in profound gratitude for the manner in which they have given me reason to hope for the future of liturgical renewal.

II.

THE WORK OF RENEWAL

LITURGICAL RENEWAL AND THE LITURGY COMMITTEE

After thirty years, the superficial enthusiasm of the early days of liturgical renewal has fallen by the wayside, and many now question whether the work of reform has stalled or failed. Certainly, the work of renewal is not for the faint-hearted or the short of breath. To accomplish such an imposing task, post-Vatican II generations will need the endurance of the long-distance runner.

Seeing the work of the parish liturgy committee in context – as part of an effort of truly historic proportions – can encourage and motivate committee members. In fact, if momentum is to be sustained over the long haul, the people of God in parishes everywhere must be convinced that their role in the work of liturgical renewal is essential.

THE WORK OF VATICAN II

We must never forget that the call for liturgical renewal came from an ecumenical council of the church. Our tradition believes deeply in the presence of the Holy Spirit guiding the church; at no time do we experience the Spirit's presence more forcefully than when all of the bishops gather in solemn assembly as pastors and teachers.

The promulgations of the bishops at Vatican II had varying degrees of importance, but they chose their most solemn form – a Constitution – for their decisions on liturgical renewal. They explicitly stated that the overall work of renewing the church is inextricably linked to the success of liturgical reform.

The Constitution on the Sacred Liturgy offers foundational principles for the renewal and the beginnings of a strategic plan to implement them. The principles themselves were the fruit of more than fifty years of scholarly and pastoral work prior to the council; they are embodied in solid, traditional Catholic theology. In principle, the liturgy should:

- nurture the full and active participation of all the faithful
- offer generous exposure to the Scripture
- differentiate among the various ministerial roles
- include music as integral to the ritual
- be adapted to the cultural genus of a people
- use ritual forms of noble simplicity and clarity
- offer symbols that speak authentically to people
- show preference for communal forms of each rite
- offer the vernacular to each people.

The plan for implementation is more sketchily delineated, but several basics are clear regarding the work to be done after the council.

THE POSTCONCILIAR ERA

1. Liturgical Books. The reform demanded the creation of an entirely new set of liturgical books that would embody the foundational principles approved at the council. Within ten years after the close of the council virtually all of those books, called the *editio typica* or the normative edition, were published.

2. Translations into Vernacular Languages. In the English-speaking world, a single group was established to ensure standardized usage everywhere. This group, known as ICEL (the International Commission on English in the Liturgy), continues to be responsible for the official translation of all liturgical books into English.

An important Vatican document concerning the process of translation was issued in 1969. It was recognized that in order to render the *editio typica* into the vernacular, newly composed texts would at times have to be created in the spirit of the Latin originals, and the books themselves would have to be rearranged in a more pastoral fashion. ICEL has consistently followed these Vatican directives by an elaborate process of study, consultation, retranslation, and pastoral editing of the books. Since both language and culture are evolutionary, this part of the reform will be ongoing.

3. Local Adaptations. Each liturgical ritual indicates who is competent to make decisions regarding local adaptations. In some instances, it is an entire episcopal conference; in others, the diocesan bishop; and, in others, the presider is given discretion to adapt in consultation with the local community. Perhaps the best example we have to date of an episcopal conference taking seriously this mandate is the work of the U.S. bishops in adapting the Rite of Christian Initiation of Adults to fit the pastoral needs of our country.

4. Liturgical Inculturation. The Constitution on the Sacred Liturgy envisions the Roman liturgy eventually undergoing a far-reaching process of assimilation according to the native genius of various peoples and cultures. Only dimly understood at the Vatican Council itself, the phenomenon of inculturation concerns not only liturgical forms but the very way in which the church proclaims the gospel to different peoples, how it understands and expresses its faith in theological categories. Needless to say, this process has barely begun.

THE WORK OF THE LOCAL PARISH

Such background information may be helpful to parish liturgy committees seeking to understand their work in a broader perspective. After such a hierarchical description of the process of liturgical renewal, however, one might feel as if having a place at the base of such a large pyramid carries little significance in the grand scheme of things. Nothing could be farther from the truth!

So far I have described merely the external structures of liturgical reform. Much more important for its eventual success is the interior renewal that must accompany structural reform at every step. Ultimately, when we speak of liturgical renewal we are talking about what happens in local parishes throughout the world, day in and day out, Sunday after Sunday. Liturgical renewal takes place not in revised books or theologically correct directives from on high, but in the hearts and lives of ordinary believers in ordinary parishes, gathering regularly to worship in Spirit and in Truth.

The work of a parish liturgy committee is as crucial for the success of Vatican II's call to reform as is the work of the local bishop or the nation's episcopal conference. Parishes must develop the skills for good liturgical celebration. Parishioners must assimilate the meaning of "full and active participation." Families and parishes must instill in their members the interior dispositions – of hospitality, gratitude, reverence, repentance, and so forth – essential for good celebrations.

Too often the momentum of liturgical renewal is being slowed, stopped, and in some cases even reversed. The forces that resist Vatican II's call for renewal are many.

From the beginning, some have rejected the direction taken by the council (dare we say by the Holy Spirit?). Thirty years after the promulgation of the *Constitution on the Sacred Liturgy*, institutional inertia has set in at many levels of our church, sometimes among those who had hoped the hard work of reform would be over by now. Others, who would push ahead with reform, experience fear in the current church atmosphere, quick to punish what is perceived as "liberal" innovation. Finally, apart from sinister ideological considerations or the grand forces of bureaucratic lethargy, there is the unadorned fact that people find it hard to cope with the demands of a renewal that will take generations to accomplish. Human nature resists change simply because it is change; change requires a kind of dying.

The primary work of the parish liturgy committee, then, is to keep working, faithfully and with great perseverance. The vision of a revitalized church, worshipping with renewed fervor, must be kept alive in the local parish. The liturgy committee must be the patient locus for training ministers for a variety of liturgical roles. It must prepare celebrations according to the vision of renewal put forth in the documents of Vatican II. It must plan and coordinate celebrations of vitality and creative energy. It must study carefully the foundational principles of the reform so as to distinguish liturgical backsliding from prudent implementation.

Most of all, the liturgy committee must be the place at the heart of a parish where the deep spirit of renewed worship of God is fostered. If the links between liturgy and life are not understood by committee members, what hope is there for the parish at large? If the committee members see no connection between Eucharist and social justice, who will challenge a parish's tendencies to self-absorption? If the liturgy committee has no sense of the beautiful, or of the importance of an environment that invites a community to worship, then how will we ever attract artists to beautify our celebrations? If parish liturgy committees abandon the effort for renewal, then and only then will the reform of Vatican II have failed.

THE TRIDENTINE MASS AND LITURGICAL REFORM

Not long ago the religion section of *The Washington Post* ran a full-page article about the resurgence of interest among Catholics in the so-called "Tridentine Mass." According to the report, efforts of traditionalists, such as the Illinois-based group "Coalition in Support of Ecclesia Dei" have spawned more than 175 groups nationwide who regularly schedule Latin Masses. That number, while small, is still significant. First, it gives pastoral ministers reason to make sure they know well – and can clarify for any who ask them – the differences between the Tridentine Mass and the Mass celebrated according to the Vatican II reforms. Second, it furnishes an occasion to review the history leading up to the reform and some current efforts to revivify it.

IS THE REFORMED MASS REALLY AN IMPROVEMENT?

Bishops, pastors, and liturgists agree that many who yearn for the prayerfulness of the old Latin liturgy have not yet been offered clear and convincing proof that the principles of renewal actually "work." They may have observed Scripture poorly proclaimed and haltingly preached, liturgical music too rarely inspiring, minimalistic or insipid use of the primary liturgical symbols, assemblies lacking the most rudimentary understanding of the crucial role which is theirs, and celebrations too cerebral, wordy, or sluggish.

Little wonder, then, that traditionalists seek a return to what they remember as a more prayerful and majestic experience of worship. The sense of religious mystery, which permeated the cavernous interiors of grand old churches while the priest offered the Holy Sacrifice of the Mass, provided a contact with God that is sorely lacking in many contemporary parishes.

How are we to respond to those who believe that the fault lies with the reform, not with those who have implemented it poorly? The answer, it seems, lies with a credible explanation of the theological and pastoral values Vatican II sought to embody in its mandate for liturgical renewal. We need to set forth clearly and persuasively how the Eucharist of Vatican II is meant to provide a renewed experience of worship for those who fully implement its vision.

As the church's official act of worship, the Mass is public and communal by nature. It is not the personal prayer of the priest, nor is it a time for individual believers to engage in private devotion. The renewed ritual seeks to express more clearly the communal and public nature of the Eucharist by asserting that the "all the faithful should be led to that full, conscious, and active participation" in the ritual action "is the aim to be considered before all else" (*Constitution on the Sacred Liturgy*, 14).

The prayerfulness of the Tridentine Mass is beyond dispute, but it was achieved in large measure by a ritual format that suggested the Eucharist was the personal prayer of the priest (expressed by the phrase "Father's Mass") and that the faithful most fruitfully "attended" by engaging in their own prayerful devotions (reciting the rosary or other prayers). The Mass of Vatican II seeks to elicit the "full and active participation of all" by a ritual format that is more consistent with communal prayer. When the reformed Mass engages the assembly in a strong act of common worship, no one could suggest that the spirit of prayer is lacking, even though the expression of worship bears little resemblance to that of the Tridentine Mass.

The shift from Latin to the vernacular was among the most significant changes of Vatican II. Traditionalists rightly point out the aura of mystery evoked by using a language few can understand. The inability of worshipers to understand a prayer in which they are to engage "fully and actively," however, required the shift to the vernacular. Being able to sing and offer spoken response in one's own language makes possible a level of personal engagement that a Latin liturgy simply cannot rival, despite its solemnity and beauty.

One of the most important principles of Vatican II's project for reform was that the faithful need and deserve to be nourished on a richer diet of Scripture. Because the Scripture is foundational to all Christian faith, the council called for Catholics to develop a "sweet and living love for sacred Scripture" (CSL, #24). Nowhere does the Mass of Vatican II more clearly improve upon the Tridentine Mass. Thanks to an expanded, three-year cycle of lectionary readings, the treasures of the Bible are lavishly offered to the faithful in the reformed Mass. The council also encouraged priests to preach homilies based on the Scriptural texts proclaimed at Mass.

Historical factors at work over many centuries resulted in the priest taking to himself some roles that originally and more properly belonged to a variety of ministers within the liturgical assembly. The council's understanding of ministry, for example, asserts that *all* the baptized (not just the ordained) are "a priestly people" whose mission is to offer God fitting worship.

The distinction between the common priesthood and the ministerial priesthood can be threatened in two ways: when the baptized seek roles that properly belong to the ordained or when the ordained keep for themselves roles that are proper to the laity.

In the Tridentine Mass, the faithful are often relegated to a passive stance, denying their baptismal priesthood as well as the liturgical roles by which it is properly expressed. The Mass of Vatican II seeks to restore a proper, balanced differentiation of roles, where all members of the assembly are called upon to do all and only that which is proper to their particular status. The designation of specific parts for the entire assembly or for cantors or lectors, for example, is consistent with that principle.

Supporters of the Tridentine Mass point out that the unchanging uniformity of its celebration in every time and place is a great strength. While there is a value to such consistency, there are alternative values achieved by the flexibility of the reformed Mass. The variety of options in prayer, music, Scripture and ritual actions, for example, permits adaptation to the unique genius of different peoples, previously an impossibility given the rigidity of the Tridentine Mass. Also, the reformed liturgy's ability to incorporate elements of various people's culture into their worship allows them to express faith in a way that resonates with other cherished values at the core of their experience. Variety of prayer and Scripture also offers greater theological richness and helps hold the attention of participants.

Vatican II's restoration of the Prayer of the Faithful to the liturgy is a remarkable example of how the revised Mass can enrich the experience of the faithful. It allows urgently felt needs to be addressed regularly and reinforces the power of the community's prayer. The connection between Eucharist and daily life is highlighted by capturing the immediacy of people's concerns. The council directed that the structure include prayer for the church, the world, those afflicted and suffering, and particular local needs, guaranteeing a balanced horizon of concern within this prayer.

The Tridentine Mass emphasized the sacrificial dimensions of the Eucharist. The priest, back turned to the people, stood before God as mediator offering sacrifice on behalf of the people. While the revised Mass is no less a sacrifice in essence, its ritual shape does bring to the fore another dimension of the Eucharist: its character as a sacred meal.

The council understood that the Mass is called a "sacrifice" not because it resembles the sacrificial ritual of the Temple, but because it is a sacramental representation of a sacred meal. The *meaning* of that ritual meal, not its ritual format, is identical with Jesus' own sacrifice on the cross.

The priest's stance at the table, facing the assembly in a posture of invitation, evokes the Lord's command at the Last Supper: "Take and eat; take and drink."

The council further highlighted the meal character in teaching that a "more perfect form of participation" is achieved when the faithful communicate from elements consecrated at "the same sacrifice" (CSL, #55) rather than, as had often been the custom with the Tridentine Mass, from hosts reserved in the tabernacle. The encouragement to communicate under the elements of both bread and wine is another example of how the Mass of Vatican II emphasizes the Eucharist as "a Paschal banquet in which Christ is consumed" (CSL, #47) in a more vivid way than did the Tridentine Mass.

HISTORICAL PERSPECTIVE

How, exactly, did the church move from the Tridentine Mass to the reformed Mass? The liturgical reforms mandated by the fathers of Vatican II were hardly the result of sudden enthusiasm. The renewal started in the nineteenth century and, by the opening of Vatican II, was already mature in its careful scholarship. The council fathers were well-informed, they deliberated prayerfully, and they discussed the *Constitution on the Sacred Liturgy* thoroughly before approving it overwhelmingly (2,147 yes votes, of 2,152 votes cast) on December 4, 1963. They were convinced that "Zeal for the promotion and restoration of the sacred liturgy is rightly held to be a sign of the providential dispositions of God in our time, and as a movement of the Holy Spirit in his Church" (CSL, #43).

THE 'LIMITED RESTORATION'

In the days immediately following the promulgation of that historic document, it seemed that the church had embarked on a whole new era in its liturgical life. Thirty years later, however, the Vatican has made provision for a "limited restoration" of the very Mass the council fathers decreed should be reformed. What happened?

Pope John Paul II took this step in 1984 in an offer to the followers of Archbishop Lefevbre (and again in 1988, in the *Motu Proprio Ecclesia Dei*). The pope had hoped to lead the Lefevbreites back from the brink of a schism (though, as is well known, he was unable to and Lefevbre was ultimately excommunicated). Similarly, in 1990 Cardinal Mayer, the head of the Pontifical Commission *Ecclesia Dei*, urged the bishops of the world to give more generous permission for celebrating the Tridentine Mass. Yet his letter, too, was published in the same restricted context as the pope's action. *Ecclesia Dei* itself had been established by the pope specifically "for the purpose of facilitating full ecclesial communion of [those] . . . linked in various ways to the society founded by Archbishop Lefevbre" (*ED*, 6a).

Since 1990, however, traditionalists have mounted a campaign to apply the norms of *Ecclesia Dei* broadly – to all who request a restoration of the Tridentine Mass for any reason whatsoever.

Meanwhile, as is evident from the *Post* article, a public misperception is growing that Catholics have two choices of equal value: the Tridentine Mass or the Mass reformed according to Vatican II. Unfortunately, that choice is misconstrued as a matter of individual taste or spiritual preference. In effect, the normative force of Vatican II's entire liturgical reform risks becoming compromised.

WHAT'S AT STAKE NOW?

Few would object to the special pastoral provisions the pope offered to the followers of Archbishop Lefevbre in order to keep them from schism. Yet the proscriptions for celebrating the Tridentine Mass are narrow, not broad. Elsewhere the pope has shown a vigorous commitment to work for the full implementation of the Vatican II reforms, which are also incumbent upon all members of the church.

The church must recommit itself to embrace fully the hard work of reform and renewal, aware that only future generations will see the vision fully realized. What is needed is deep faith that the community's worship truly is of supreme importance and that in some real way the renewal of the church itself is at stake in our attempts at liturgical reform.

WE BELIEVE

To bolster the pope's position and that of the council fathers among the public at large, a group called "We Believe" (in the teachings of the Second Vatican Council) has recently organized a national effort to collect signatures on a document expressing support for the liturgical renewal of Vatican II.

Substantive liturgical renewal has never been accomplished easily or within a single generation. Liturgical historians have observed that several factors are required for liturgical reform to succeed:

- a commitment to its importance by the church at large
- painstaking and persevering effort – by theorists and practitioners alike – to promulgate it and practice it
- strong support from those in positions of leadership.

Liturgical leaders are becoming increasingly vocal in recent times, insisting that if the work of Vatican II's liturgical reform is to succeed, then a firm commitment to its importance is needed at every level of the church.

Reflecting sober judgment in the face of the traditionalist resurgence, they admit that perhaps proponents of reform have been much too naive about the price of renewal, too quick to tire and move on, too willing to settle for something less than deep and lasting reform, and too timid or fearful when met with resistance.

For them, spreading efforts to reinstall the Tridentine Mass have served as a wake up call. More and more theologians, liturgists, and pastoral leaders are asking the bishops to stand up firmly and forcefully on behalf of the *aggiornamento* for which the Vatican Council was convoked.

WHAT IS NEEDED?

It would help the reform movement if the following conditions were met throughout the church at large:
- seminaries and schools of theology need to give a much higher priority to liturgical formation
- national centers of pastoral liturgy and the bishops' own staff offices need additional funding and invigorated leadership
- trends to curtail or eliminate diocesan-level agencies for liturgical renewal must be reversed
- parishes must redouble their efforts to move beyond dull Sunday morning rituals, becoming communities of authentic celebration where full, conscious, and active participation is the norm.

LITURGY COMMITTEES

One of the most prominent legacies the Second Vatican Council has bequeathed to today's parish is the council/committee structure. Implementation of the liturgical reforms of the last three decades has often struggled as much with these fledgling structures as with the changes themselves. Vatican II launched us on the project of liturgical reform, often in vehicles ill-suited to accomplish that complex task. And even today, the ongoing work of accomplishing the "people's work" (liturgy) is frequently entrusted to committees whose structures and working procedures have received little critical scrutiny. Such naiveté is a luxury we cannot and should not afford. The price exacted in poor results and frustrated workers is too high to continue paying.

The fall of the year is the time when parish communities gear up their programs and their committees. It is also a good time to review some of the obvious "basics," which are all too easily overlooked in the hectic pace of parish activity. What follows are some fundamental components of a well functioning parish liturgy committee.

CLARITY OF PURPOSE, SCOPE, AND TASK

One of the most common pitfalls experienced by liturgy committees is confusion about their purpose, their scope, and their responsibilities. The range of options is considerable, and there need be no *a priori* suppositions as to what is appropriate in any setting. In fact, negotiating its boundaries is often an important stage in developing a mature committee. Is the committee set up for review and evaluation, or is it to be involved in direct liturgy planning? Is the committee's scope directed toward the Sunday Eucharist or particular Sunday liturgies, or does it include all parish liturgies? Does the committee have the right to comment on the perform- ances of the personnel in the liturgy, and if so, does that include or exclude the clergy? Stated clarity in the committee's purpose, in the breadth of its authority, and in its concrete tasks will avoid the problems that come when these are not stated – the substitution of members' subjective expectations in each area.

Members of the committee need to consider where policies should originate, where they are reviewed for com- ment, and who officially promulgates them. Developing an overall vision of the liturgical life of the parish seems to be an attractive option for many committees. This necessitates subsidiary functions, such as needs assessment, evaluation, and so forth. Responsibility for development and coordina- tion of liturgical ministries may or may not be part of a committee's competence. Likewise, the task of planning and preparing for liturgical seasons and feasts might be done as part of the committee's work or fall to another group. Whatever decisions are made as to the purpose of a given committee, they should be realistic and manageable and reflect the consensus of its members. Part of the realism is the recognition that major authority and responsibility for the liturgy is already in the hands of the pastor and the one who presides at the liturgy. Another part of the realism is the committee's authority relative to other parish groups, like the council and the staff.

A WRITTEN CHARTER

Once a committee has reached the desired clarity, it is important to put this in writing. Consensus is a fragile thing, and shared understanding can be even more elusive. For all of the tedium and pain that is involved in hammering out a written document, the rewards are well worth the effort. Every committee needs to have some sort of written charter. It matters little whether this takes the form of a mission statement, a constitution, guidelines, or merely procedural rules. What is important is that it capture and reflect accurately the clarity of purpose that has been reached in the committee. This serves the invaluable functions of reminding members of the decisions reached, helping new members to understand their role, and communicating to other parish structures realistic expectations of the liturgy committee.

STRUCTURE AND MEMBERSHIP

We state the obvious in saying that form must follow function, but it is surprising how often committees fail to take into account this basic truth. A careful, critical assessment must be made to decide what is the best structure to accomplish the purpose of the committee. The delicate balance between being too large to work efficiently and too small to muster needed resources is always a challenge to maintain. Most have found that a number between eight and sixteen seems most workable for the kinds of responsibilities usually entrusted to a liturgy committee.

The issue of committee membership is important. Should the committee be representative? If so, of whom? The community at large? Each liturgical ministry? Particular areas of expertise needed for its task? These are some of the questions that will have to be examined and resolved in order to come up with a workable formula for membership. Many parishes have found that the principle of subsidiarity works well in determining these issues. Working subgroups, either *ad hoc* task groups or subcommittees, are entrusted with particular areas of responsibility and only report back to the larger committee as needed. In addition to avoiding an overly large committee, this has the added benefit of involving more people actively in the liturgical infrastructure of the parish.

GOOD MEETINGS

Parish staff and volunteers in our generation need a whole new set of skills in order to carry on the work of the gospel in today's world. One of the most important skills for those who are committee members is learning how to conduct good meetings. Ours is the age of the small group, and like it or not, we must learn about and be sensitive to the "rules" of good group process. Most committees will not need the formality of Robert's Rules of Order, but every group will profit from a clear decision about its procedural rules. Good meetings do not just happen; their agenda must be carefully planned. That means some thoughtful decisions must be made in advance about priorities and how best to formulate issues for group discussion. As a general rule, the more carefully constructed the agenda, the better the quality of the meeting will be. Good agendas list the topic, who will present it, whether it is for "information only, discussion, or decision," as well as the amount of time that will be spent on each item. In mature committees, there is a balance between task orientation and relational concerns, and every participant – not just the chairperson – takes responsibility for the quality of the discussion. The question of who sets the agenda, and how items can be placed on it, is one that needs clarity and consensus. Good meetings also include careful documentation through the provision of minutes, supporting records, and so forth.

FORMATION OF MEMBERS

A healthy liturgy committee will attend to two aspects of the formation needs of its members: spirituality and competence. Because of the nature of the issues with which a liturgy committee deals, it is absolutely essential that its work be conducted in an atmosphere of faith. Every meeting should include a time of prayer – not perfunctory words quickly mumbled at the beginning, but authentic prayer.

In addition it is ideal to have other experiences throughout the year that are specifically geared to nourishing members for their work in shaping the prayer of God's people. Many Catholic people have little experience with liturgy other than the Sunday Eucharist. Opening up to them other parts of the church's spiritual heritage, for example, through attendance at ordinations or the rite of election or other liturgies not commonly seen in a parish, can expand their awareness of what is possible and appropriate.

The second level of formation that seems essential has to do with competence: the knowledge and skills necessary to do the work. Members are not necessarily expected to have theological training in the liturgical sciences, but they should have an expectation that they will grow in the knowledge and the "art" of the liturgy. Some reading should be assigned and expected; staff or outside resources should be provided;

and in-service, peer interactions that help members to grow in competence should be encouraged.

These points are some of the "basics" for a vital and effective parish liturgy committee. Other elements could easily have been added, but we have chosen to stick to a few of the most fundamental components in the hope of highlighting what seems most important. As with so many other areas of life, it seems that if only we devote time, attention, and energy to something, it will improve. We should recognize that this is true of parish liturgy committees as well and so be encouraged to make an appropriate commitment of our best resources.

THE BOOKS WE USE AT WORSHIP

At a recent gathering of liturgical leaders, a major speaker mentioned that in preparing for his talk he conducted an informal survey of nearby parishes to see how extensively the revised sacramental rituals were being implemented. He discovered that a number of the parishes did not even have copies of all the ritual books (the order of Christian funerals, for example), books that have been revised and promulgated for several years. This simple reality-check had brought home to him the importance of not taking anything for granted regarding the liturgical renewal.

That story prompts me to make the following suggestion: the parish liturgy committee might do well to evaluate the books used at worship: What are they? What's in them? For whom are they intended? How well is the parish using them?

WHAT ARE THEY?

The Second Vatican Council set out to reform Catholic worship by mandating a complete revision of the church's "liturgical library" in light of basic principles elaborated in the Constitution on the Sacred Liturgy. Many of those books are published today as multivolume works, but in the official schema of the reform the list is short: the divine office (liturgy of the hours), the Roman ritual, the Roman missal, the ceremonial of bishops, the Roman pontifical, the Roman martyrology, and several volumes containing official Latin chants.

The first three of these are books with which parish liturgy committees ought to be familiar. The liturgy of the hours usually is divided seasonally, with a book of supplementary readings published separately. The Roman ritual contains many sacramental rites, as well as the book of blessings, the rite of religious profession, the order of Christian funerals, and more. The Roman missal also appears currently in multiple volumes: the lectionary, the book of Gospels, the sacramentary, and the Roman gradual.

The decision to issue the various liturgical books as separate volumes is more than a simple editorial choice made by publishers. It is part of a deliberate restoration of the various liturgical ministries which, during the Middle Ages, had gradually been absorbed into the priestly office. The reform of Vatican II intended to bolster the integrity and complementarity of the various liturgical ministries by providing each ministry with a book specifically designed for those who exercise it. We are still at an early stage of such a vision, however, evident in the many texts that contain material rightly belonging to other ministers. The sacramentary, for example, is published with entrance and communion verses, and the lectionary has both the cantor's psalmody and the deacon's gospel readings.

One basic responsibility of the parish liturgy committee is to know what the books of the Roman liturgical reform are, how they have been published for use in separate volumes, and where they are available. It might also be appropriate for the committee to ensure that these books, in their most recently authorized version, are on the parish shelves and accessible to those responsible for their use.

WHAT IS IN THEM?

Basic elements are found in most of the liturgical books, beginning with the "Introduction" (which translates the Latin term "*praenotanda*").

- *Introduction.* In the reformed books of Vatican II, the introduction is an extremely important section that contains the theological vision of the rite, pastoral notes on preparing for and celebratng the rite, and provisions for the adaptation of the rite at various levels. Proper use of any ritual presumes a careful reading and study of its introduction. Members of the parish liturgy committee as well as presiders will find such reading helpful. The introduction also may include important pastoral adaptations and developments by the conference of bishops for use in specific regions.
- *Rubrics.* Each book contains rubrics or ritual directions (usually printed in red) indicating some of the basic choreography of the celebration, where improvisation is allowed, and where the text is to be followed as given.
- *Text.* This "script" contains ancient and venerable prayers as well as texts newly composed for the needs of the third millennium, parts considered essential to the integrity of the rite, and other sections that are optional and variable. Like any script, the words must be carefully read and studied before appropriate choices can be made in preparing the actual celebration.
- *Alternatives.* Each book contains a section of alternative materials (prayers, songs, Scripture readings) that enhance variety and assist in selecting material for specific occasions.

It may take a liturgy committee several years to understand deeply what is contained in each of the books that comprise the post-Vatican II liturgical library, so the learning project is an ongoing one. When revised editions appear, new developments must be assimilated and the new understandings behind them implemented. In a few years, for example, an entirely new edition of the sacramentary will be published, decisively shaping Catholic eucharistic worship for the next generation.

FOR WHOM ARE THEY INTENDED?

In every celebration the various ministers are to do "all but only" what is properly theirs to do. It helps to know for whom the liturgical books are intended. The ideal celebration is a symphony in many parts, with the full and active participation of all persons present according to their respective ministries. Certain books belong in the hands of many people during the preparation stage, but once the celebration begins each ministry needs only the material that is proper to it and necessary for the accomplishment of its ministry.

For that reason many liturgists support the publication of daily or Sunday missals with the full texts of the liturgical celebrations so that members of the assembly and specific ministers may prepare, but they oppose the assembly's use of such materials during the celebration itself.

One of the lingering symptoms of the medieval assimilation of liturgical roles by the clergy is that the liturgical books are still the exclusive domain of the ordained. Many of these books can and should be accessible to others: Eucharistic ministers to the homebound, for example, should have copies of the rite of anointing and pastoral care of the sick. The order of Christian funerals should be available to families preparing for the funeral of a loved one and to those who lead prayer at the time of death. Lectors should study the introduction to the lectionary with care, and engaged couples should study the entire rite of marriage, not just selected readings from the lectionary. Catechumenal team members must be intimately familiar with the rite of Christian initiation of adults. Smaller versions of the book of blessings and the liturgy of the hours ought to be well-worn books in Catholic homes.

The parish liturgy committee ought to ensure that all those for whom the liturgical books are intended have them and know how to use them.

HOW WELL ARE WE USING THEM?

In many ways this question is asked on every page of this volume. Because the liturgical books contain virtually the entire vision of the Vatican II reform, parishes must return time and again to these books to shape and improve their own vision and practice. But before the work of liturgical adaptation and inculturation can go forward, local parishes must master the foundational realities contained in these books.

Unfortunately, thirty years after the council, some parishes continue to baptize adults using the old ritual for children; some have failed to adopt changes in eucharistic practice and still, for example, distribute Communion on Sunday using hosts consecrated at a previous celebration. Scripture should never be proclaimed from a tattered missalette, nor should the sacrament of penance be celebrated in the musty confessionals common before the council.

The challenge facing the parish liturgy committee is to see to it that both the spirit and the content of the renewed liturgical books is practiced in everyday ways that shape the spiritual lives of all those at worship. That task may well outlive us all, but the privileged work of beginning it is ours.

Preparing the Assembly for Liturgy

Great musicians regularly spend many hours each day practicing their craft. Award-winning actors and actresses pay handsome salaries to drama coaches, who work with them over and over to improve their skills. Youngsters in my parish are up before dawn every day to swim for more than an hour in the hope of enhancing their performance in the next swim meet. Directors of television shows with audience participation would never dream of going on air without first warming up the audience. My sister-in-law regularly "practices" new recipes on her family before serving them to company. It seems our culture is replete with examples of those who understand the importance of careful preparation in order to perform well.

PRACTICE MAKES PERFECT

That familiar idea has parallels in liturgical life. Remarkably, what seems so obvious and uncontested in some parts of daily life sometimes appears innovative (even unreasonable) when applied to the ritual performance we call Sunday Mass. For example, the primacy of the ministry of the assembly at Sunday Eucharist is often stressed by liturgists, yet the notion of helping the assembly to prepare for their ministry still sounds strangely new. The suggestion that a community might challenge its members, holding them accountable for their responsibility to prepare for their ministry, sounds downright unrealistic! Why?

No choirs or soloists worth their salt would walk on stage for a performance without having learned their part well in advance and warmed up their vocal chords before beginning. In spite of this obvious necessity, it is still common to see song leaders announce the opening song and expect the Sunday assembly to perform its musical role with absolutely no time to practice or warm up their voices. Taking time before Mass for the assembly to rehearse, learn new music, and just exercise their vocal chords is still regarded by many as an intrusion to be resentfully tolerated.

Liturgical leaders bear responsibility for awakening and forming attitudes that will create positive expectations and openness in this regard. We should look forward to the time when parishioners would complain if they were deprived of their musical preparation before Mass starts!

PREPARING THE ASSEMBLY FOR MASS

Many presiders use their remarks after the opening greeting to focus the assembly's attention and help prepare their minds and hearts for the celebration. In some places, a more extensive effort is made, prior to the opening song, to engage the assembly in ways that will prepare them for full participation. Frequently done in conjunction with the music rehearsal, preparation can take the form of remarks about the scriptural or seasonal themes in the day's celebration, the musical texts and why they were chosen, or other events and experiences that contribute to the life situation of the community on that occasion. Such an effort might also include some thought-provoking questions or dialogue with members of the assembly. In whatever fashion it is done, the point is that thoughtful and attentive participation in the liturgy is expected of all present.

DEVELOPING RITUAL COMPETENCY

From time to time, liturgical leaders need to address a more basic kind of formation, which will enhance the ritual competency of the parish at large. This fancy term refers to the predispositions worshipers bring to the celebration, which better equip them to participate in the symbolic language of our rituals. What is intended here is attitude and value formation, as well as specific knowledge and skills necessary to enter into the spirit of Christian worship. A parish liturgy team might profit from a brainstorming session to identify areas where formation is needed, followed by another session to develop strategies to accomplish the goals identified.

For example, a parish may be characterized by rushing through the liturgy of the word. In a brainstorming session, the liturgy team might recognize, consequently, how minimal is the assembly's capacity for reflective silence. Various strategies could be generated as part of a long-range plan to increase the assembly's capacity to reflect quietly together on the readings after they are proclaimed. These strategies could include adult education courses on Scripture, revelation, and how faith comes as a response to invitation. Someone could work with lectors, cantors, and presiders to increase gradually the amount of quiet time between their proclamations; quieting exercises – such as measured breathing or other centering techniques – could be introduced into the song rehearsal at the start of Mass. Parish groups that use Scripture-based faith sharing could be worked with to increase their members' ability to sit quietly together in prayer after reading Scripture; popular explanations in the bulletin could explain the goal to the parish at large and offer suggestions on how to become more aware of one's capacity for contemplative silence. Catechists in the religious education program could be approached to solicit their support and creative ideas about how to work with children; and many other such strategies could be developed as well.

PARENTS LAY THE FOUNDATION

The notion of ritual competency is an especially important one for parents. A parish would be well-advised to make particular efforts to help parents understand how the family is the setting in which a child's fundamental level of ritual competency is established. Family rituals of togetherness, reconciliation, festive celebration, and so forth lay the groundwork for explicitly religious ritual. Familiarity with primary

Christian symbols in their secular and religious dimensions (bread, wine, fire, water, oil, touch) is learned first at home. It is also in the home that basic attitudes are formed toward church, participation in worship, reverence for the bodilessness of sacramentals, and many other aspects of ritual competency.

Parents prepare their children for worship in many other ways besides teaching them how to say their prayers. The imaginative world of childhood is a broadly foundational period of formation, as youngsters, by story and familiar family rituals, gradually construct a world of meaning through symbols. Of course, in order to do this task as well as possible, parents themselves must be comfortable with family and religious rituals. They must be willing to enter again into the simplicity of a child's world of wonder and awe, to experience the reverence of a child discovering nature for the first time, and to connect the child's experience, even in the earliest years, with the sacramental presence of God in creation and in human history. Parishes that help parents in this important aspect of spiritual formation of their children will surely reap the benefits in an adult community that is more fully empowered to worship.

LEADERSHIP AND MATERIALS

Helping an assembly prepare to celebrate better the Sunday Eucharist is an essential element of pastoral leadership. In homilies, exhortations interspersed throughout the celebration, and other teaching opportunities outside the liturgy, presiders should regularly call the community to account for how well they have prepared themselves for worship. The good will and authentic spiritual hunger that draws people to our liturgical assemblies should be assumed. If they can be taught skills that will allow them to enter more deeply into the sacred mystery of the Eucharist, their participation will surely reflect a greater degree of active involvement. Something as simple as helping people learn how to prepare the Scripture readings for the coming Sunday holds enormous potential for a more attentive and receptive celebration of the liturgy of the word.

People need access to the broad range of popular materials available that explain the scriptural texts and offer relevant questions for consideration. A half-century after the Catholic church embraced the fruits of contemporary scriptural scholarship, there is still massive scriptural illiteracy and rampant fundamentalism in many Catholics' approach to scriptural interpretation. Parishes need to take seriously their responsibility to form the faithful for an authentic hearing of the word and not settle too quickly for the pervasive ignorance of Scripture that is currently the norm in so many places.

These remarks have been directed toward the need for the assembly at large to be prepared for its role in the liturgical celebration. In fact, all of the ministries require more preparation than is currently the norm, from lectors to acolytes, from greeters to preachers. We must not rest until our church matches the expectations of our society in demanding careful preparation by all who perform important liturgical roles within the community. The specific ministry of the liturgical assembly requires more careful preparation than most parishes, so far, have given it.

FULL AND ACTIVE PARTICIPATION

In a large suburban parish in Kansas City on a recent Memorial Day, worshipers were asked to take out their car keys so that the pastor could proceed through the church and sprinkle them in a gesture of holiday blessing. What this ritual had to do with either the civil holiday or its liturgical observance is hard to determine. But apparently someone thought the action would be a good way to achieve meaningful involvement of the assembly on that occasion.

As silly as this example may sound, it reflects accurately the sort of attempts being made around the country to draw people into liturgical celebrations in ways that will be "engaging" and "relevant." The impetus for such concerns, of course, is the realization that "full and active participation by all of the people is the aim to be considered before all else" in the liturgical renewal (emphasis added, CSL, #14). This concern is legitimate; indeed, it is precisely on target. In fact, no other single principle of liturgical renewal can rival this one which has been repeated in virtually every church document on the subject throughout this century. The active engagement, both on the level of internal involvement and in terms of exterior participation, of those who come for worship is certainly our first pastoral priority.

How best to do that, however, remains the problematic issue and the source of much confusion and misguided liturgical silliness. What follows are some commonsense suggestions about ways to achieve this desired aim. Each point might well give rise to a whole series of reflections on and improvements in how our liturgy is celebrated. As an "examination of conscience," it may seem somewhat obvious. But experience has shown that the obvious is often the most easily overlooked and neglected. What are the ways, then, that we are to work toward "full and active participation"?

HOSPITALITY

The atmosphere of any gathering, especially a liturgical one, sets a mood and defines appropriate behavior far more effectively than a thousand instructions or rules will ever do. It is a simple fact that warm and welcoming environments put people at their ease and encourage them to be more expressive and interactive. This is accomplished in liturgical settings in various ways, but certainly among the most obvious is the presence of greeters or other hospitality ministers who offer a friendly hello and make all feel welcome and accepted. Similarly, the proper tone from song leaders who "warm up" the assembly or from presiders as they open the celebration, can have a decisive effect on the willingness of those gathered to participate actively.

ACOUSTICS AND VISUALS

This may seem the most basic of all points, but how often it is violated! Unless one is able to see and hear what is happening without straining, it is virtually impossible to feel a part and to participate easily. Most churches have fixed seating, but even those with flexible seating often fail to create arrangements of the space that afford a high priority to lines of sight and other spatial relationships. What is desirable is a situation that permits eye contact, not only between presider and assembly, but also between members of the assembly, the ministers, and so forth. The sound systems in many churches also defy anyone to hear without straining. When sounds are inaudible or so garbled as to be unintelligible, the inevitable result is a sense of not being part of the action. Of course, often the problem is not in the mechanics of the electronic equipment, but in those who use it. It is a rare person who is engaged and drawn into meaningful dialogue with a mumbler!

MUSICAL ACCESS

Our enlightened society now has laws requiring public gatherings to provide access to the handicapped. Since music remains the primary vehicle for congregational participation in worship, it might be well to formulate some laws of our own in this regard. Access to musical participation starts with providing those who are asked to sing with the words and the music they need. This may not always require something on paper, though in most cases it will. Occasionally a careful rehearsal will suffice to make all feel comfortable with a simple, short text. Only rarely would one expect a congregation to be able to fulfill its musical responsibilities on a Sunday morning without so much as a warm-up or rehearsal. Certainly, no self-respecting choir would think of just arriving and opening the hymnal for the first song. Yet, one frequently sees congregations treated in just that way. Wherever assemblies are asked to sing, they need a leader to prepare and lead them just as surely as does a fully trained choir – in fact, probably more so. The concept of musical access also involves such issues as the complexity of the pieces entrusted to the assembly, the musical range within which they are expected to operate, the amount of new material they must learn at any given time, as well as questions of style and taste that may be alienating to some, rather than engaging.

SILENCE

The presence of this element may surprise some, especially if it is associated with the Tridentine liturgy's imposed silence, which prohibited liturgical participation and encouraged simultaneous private devotion. Yet experience of the reformed liturgy has shown the perils of celebrations filled with noise and devoid of quiet, reflective spaces. That interior participation which Vatican II calls for and which is the absolute foundation of all other forms of external involvement can only happen where there is ample room for silence and liturgical flow. A liturgy of the word that happens in rapid-fire sequence without substantial time for reflection between readings, psalmody, and homily is one that blocks the deeper involvement of the spirit so necessary for authentic celebration.

At the risk of sounding like an old-time pastor haranguing and berating, I must say that two common features of every assembly are often the death of prayerful silence: latecomers and screaming children. We need not be rigid or intolerant of the foibles of the human condition when we insist that there are limits beyond which one ought not trespass. The situation in some parishes where latecomers effectively disrupt the entire liturgy of the word week after week is quite simply intolerable. That means it ought not to be tolerated! Similarly, we need to recognize the difference between fussy babies who distract slightly and occasionally, and those young ones whose chorus of screams makes it impossible to hear, pray, or reflect. These, too, ought not to be tolerated. What is at stake, besides good etiquette and common sense, is the very heart of an assembly's right and responsibility to worship. Our standards of silence do not have to approach those of the symphony hall, but neither should they be indistinguishable from those of the baseball park.

PREPARATION

Under this rubric one must include a variety of elements. Certainly, one way of involving the assembly more actively in the actual celebration is to see to it that there has been a prior involvement by as many as possible in the preparation for the celebration. There is a sense of ownership that results when one has helped to create an event that can be achieved in no other way. The liturgical documents have long called for including the faithful in the planning process, but this is all too often honored more in the breach than in fact. Parishes need constantly to assess whether their planning process for celebrations is available to and inclusive of a wide range of parishioners. One obvious but terribly underutilized opportunity for achieving this is the prayer of the faithful. Too often it is hurriedly dashed off by one of the priests or a too-busy staff member, rather than being the product of the faithful whose name it bears. There ought to be wordsmiths in every community with an ear to the ground of popular need and longing who can express those aspirations clearly and forcefully. It is ever so much easier to participate actively in a prayer when what is being prayed for resonates deeply in one's soul. A final way of looking at preparation as an element of active participation has to do with those group or individual activities that help to open up the meaning of the scriptural texts for a given celebration. Whether it be a study/rehearsal session for lectors or a prayer group that uses the texts of the coming Sunday for focus, such times of preparation inevitably result in higher levels of involvement and participation when the celebration actually takes place.

MINISTRIES

One of the most basic senses intended by the call for active participation has to do with use of the full range of ministries possible in any given celebration. Each person is to do all and only his or her role according to the liturgical directives, and this necessitates participation by large numbers in a variety of roles. There must be active involvement by ministers of hospitality and ushers, by lectors, acolytes, eucharistic ministers, and cantors; there should be bread bakers and artists who bring beauty, vocalists and instrumentalists, presiders and deacons, sacristans and those who launder, polish, and scrub. Most important, the assembly itself must come to be convinced that its role is truly a ministry and that its ministry is most perfectly performed by full and active participation. Not only must these ministries be actualized; they must all be performed in ways that invite full and active participation. Choirs that think their job is to perform only, and not support or invite congregational participation, should be dissolved forthwith. Presiders who still communicate that all of the others are intruders on ministry, or window dressing at best, should join the aforementioned choirs in limbo. What each and every ministry must sense is that together, and only together, can we create that symphony of praise that is truly pleasing to the Lord. There are no spectators at worship, or at least there should be none. We are all members of the band, and we do our part best when in our respective ways we give that "full and active" participation to which we are called.

When the Rubrics Allow "These or Similar Words"

Those whose liturgical memories stretch back to the days before Vatican II will recall celebrations of such precision and invariability that it was possible to know in advance every word of the ritual the celebrant would utter. In some unfortunate parishes that predictability extended even to the sermon, which emerged like clockwork from the pastor's files year after year on the appointed Sunday.

The Tridentine Mass and other sacramental rites placed a high premium on uniformity. Priests were trained carefully to screen out from their delivery any idiosyncrasies that might add a personal touch to the sacred rite. Of course, the fact that the spoken words were all in Latin was a powerful incentive not to extemporize on the assigned texts. After four hundred years of such rigid adherence to the exact letter of the Latin text, it is little wonder that priests (and the faithful) were ill-prepared for the freedom offered in the post-Vatican II liturgical rites. With the advent of rituals celebrated in the vernacular, a startling new directive appeared in our liturgical books, dictating that the celebrant speak "in these or similar words." With increasing frequency in subsequent revisions of the liturgical books, this phrase became a ubiquitous rubrical challenge to the presider's rhetorical skills.

As an aid, several sample texts from which the presider can choose often accompany the familiar wording. In some instances, entire intercessory litanies are left to be composed at the discretion of the presider (or his delegate).

EXERCISING JUDICIOUS RESTRAINT

The evolution of current liturgical practice has resulted in several ways of handling this invitation to creativity.

Some presiders rarely if ever exercise the option to supply their own words, preferring instead the security of the printed sample texts.

Others, overly confident of their own eloquence, use the opportunity to expand at length on whatever happens to be in their mind. The guiding principle seems to be, "Too much of a good thing is wonderful."

Still others (unfortunately, a minority) prepare carefully and exercise judicious restraint in personalizing the message where invited to do so by the rubrics.

That this characteristic feature of the liturgical renewal is so little or so poorly used is unfortunate indeed. Much more is at stake than variety. In fact, a great deal is at stake when one realizes the full potential this rubrical freedom offers. An important invitation is being offered: to begin, in a very simple way, the process of inculturating the classical Roman liturgical forms and texts. While a modest offer, the rubric does invite the presider to bring to the celebration the native genius of the people with whom he celebrates. By choice of imagery that resonates deeply in the soul of his people or by evoking or directing attention to matters of great moment in the local culture, the presider has the opportunity of engaging the participants at a level far deeper than might otherwise have been possible.

If we have done so poorly with this little bit entrusted to us, it is no wonder the Roman powers-that-be have been hesitant to promote further the inculturation called for in the original vision of liturgical reform.

CLARIFYING THEMATIC CONNECTIONS

A second value at issue is the opportunity to integrate disparate parts of complex liturgical rituals into a more coherent unity. For example, a presider can carefully weave phrases and images from the day's Scripture, homily, and liturgical season to make clear the thematic connections, and can repeat key ideas to great effect. Good liturgical ritual loves to echo itself, reveling in creative resonances, layering meaning upon meaning each time an image or theme is revisited. It is a service to the assembly when a skillful presider links various parts of the ritual in a meaningful fashion. Not every ear is attuned nor eye trained to recognize the connections that exist as a ritual unfolds. With measured economy, the presider's exhortations and comments can subtly but surely assist the assembly to experience the unity of the liturgical experience, its coherence and integrity.

PROVIDING SOUND LITURGICAL FORMATION

Another benefit of using such well-chosen words is that it gradually adds to the liturgical formation of the worshiping assembly. By focusing on the meaning of the developing celebration, a presider can instruct the assembly in ways that will permanently raise their level of liturgical literacy. As an opportunity for ritual catechesis, the presider's remarks are usually positioned at strategic points. Over a long period of time, the remarks can significantly enhance the community's worship experience.

How might a presider (and community) reap the full benefit of that innocent phrase, "in these or similar words"? A first step might be to identify all of the opportunities where such creative work is called for. A careful reading of the General Instruction to the Roman Missal and of the eucharistic rubrics themselves will quickly generate an impressive list. A look at each of the other sacramental rites will further confirm how important are these opportunities to personalize the ritual.

Once that list is compiled, it would be helpful for the presider to analyze exactly what forms of discourse are at issue. One will notice that the range and variety of forms is substantial: words of greeting, admonitions, questions posed to the assembly or specific participants, tropes, intercessory litanies, commentaries on the meaning of liturgical units, instructions addressed to recipients of the sacramental actions – all of these forms of expression, and more, are left to the creative ability of the presider, who is urged to speak "in these or similar words." Having identified the available options, presiders could profit from gathering a small group to talk through some basic strategies that will guide his creative efforts over a period of time. Are there particular points in the Sunday Eucharist, for example, when the assembly appears to need guidance or formation? Have certain opportunities hitherto been neglected? And (if trust levels are high enough between the group and the presider) does the presider have any unconscious speech patterns that stand in need of improvement? Honest feedback that will help the presider heighten his awareness of how he is coming across can be invaluable. Is he too verbose? Is he failing to make enough use of the options to use his own words? Such issues need to be addressed frankly if the presider is to improve his skills.

PREPARING FOR THE RITUAL

The presider will need to build into his pattern of preparation for liturgical celebrations specific attention on the ways he will make use of the creative options under consideration. Depending on his skill at extemporaneous speaking, preparation will require more or less time and effort. He will want to think through the major themes he wishes to weave into the celebration at different points. He may also identify certain images that tie together or highlight various elements of the celebration. In some cases, he may actually wish to write out the exact wording of his intervention. The rubric "in these or similar words" does not intend spontaneous, off-the-cuff remarks when it invites the presider to substitute his own words for what is in the official text. Rather, it invites careful, thoughtful alternatives leading to deeper and better prayer.

The presider's role in addressing this task is not unlike that of the poet. The poet knows the power of speech and labors with love to find the precise word that will both convey meaning and evoke a response in the hearer. The poet's challenge is to say more with less in leading readers/hearers into worlds of meaning. So must presiders consider their task as they lead the assembly in prayer Our liturgical texts are often accused of being too wordy and filled with dry, un-imaginative words. Blessed is the presider (and his assembly) who can find just the right turn of phrase to awaken fresh interest in those gathered for prayer. When that happens, the presider is instrumental in allowing the Word Incarnate to take flesh once more in human speech. The presider's words evoke mystery. And, in so doing, he utters words that save!

III.

LITURGICAL SYMBOLS

LITURGICAL SYMBOLS: A PRACTICAL APPROACH

Liturgists regularly insist that effective celebration requires full, robust symbols that are allowed to speak directly, clearly, and with all their expressive power. Liturgy, like all rituals, involves choreographed patterns of symbols, put together in ways that are meaningful to the participants. If the symbols are muted and timidly done, then the message of the celebration is spoken with less conviction and impact. The challenge often faced by liturgical planners is how to free the primary symbols embedded in our rituals so that they will touch those gathered in deep and lasting ways.

There is a hint in Vatican II's *Constitution on the Sacred Liturgy* as to the urgency of this task. In paragraph number seven, the document declares that "in the liturgy, human sanctification . . . is effected in ways appropriate to each of these signs." In view of this, liturgical planning must necessarily concern itself with the primary symbols in the ritual and attempt to allow their natural meaningful expression. Our "sanctification" depends on it.

PREPARING THE LITURGIES OF HOLY WEEK

The complexity and sheer volume of issues involved in those rituals can easily bewilder and overwhelm even the most determined planners. Faced with the enormity of the chal-

41

lenge, planning teams are often tempted to fall back into a merely logistical support role. The creative dimension of planning then easily gives way to a review of the rubrics and some scattered attempts to "dress up" the rite with symbolic elements that are peripheral if not downright extraneous.

I would like to suggest a practical, down-to-earth approach to liturgical planning that should help to avoid such errors. It may seem to belabor the obvious, but my proposal is that planners begin with first things first. This simple truth is one of those "forests" so often difficult to spot through the trees. By "first things" I mean the primary symbolic elements in any rite. What are the foundational symbols around which the ritual revolves? What are the actions and objects that, in a sense, define the rite's basic meaning? Identify these first, and begin planning with a reflection on what they are about and how they may be freed to "speak" with eloquence and power.

An illustration of this suggestion seems in order. A planning team charged with preparing the Easter vigil celebration would first try to identify the major symbols in each part of that evening's complex flow of events. Probably the group's list would eventually include fire, word proclaimed, water and oil, bread and wine. Each of these in turn would then be discussed. What aspect of the many-layered meanings inherent in the symbol should be allowed major emphasis? Should the fire speak of its capacity to burn and destroy, or warm and give light? Which experience of the fire seems most important to highlight – the new fire, the Paschal candle, or the tapers of the assembly? What is it about water that we need most to examine at the vigil? Its power to quench thirst and offer cool refreshment? Its cleansing? Its destructive force or its role as womb of life? Time spent exploring such questions is invaluable and should stimulate creativity in the group.

Out of this process should emerge a sense of emphasis, a "feel" for which elements are primary and which issues require the group's further energy and attention. I am not suggesting any attempt to limit the symbols' meaning – as if to say, "We've decided this year the new fire will symbolize warmth in the cold and dark, nothing else!" Instead, I am suggesting a way of approaching the planning task that will put planners in touch with the primal powers of our primary symbols. Then, strategies can be discussed and formulated so that the choreography of the rite will permit that primal power to be experienced by the assembly.

For example, discussion of the element of fire may convince the planners that everyone needs to have a more immediate experience of fire than has occurred in previous years. No more tiny charcoal braziers in the vestibule. This year, we gather at the edge of the back parking lot around a huge bonfire. In addition to involving the scout troop in the challenge of building and controlling a large enough blaze to warm five hundred onlookers, the decision may put everyone in touch with memories of campfires long forgotten, good feelings of friends gathered together to share stories and sing songs. The experience of such a fire, in fact, will establish a mood that is ideal for the stories and songs of the liturgy of the word.

Out of the group's decision to develop more fully the fire symbol will come other secondary considerations and decisions. Perhaps the decorative dressing of the Paschal candle with incense and stylus tracings will seem superfluous in such a setting, a weak symbolic attempt that is best discarded. Perhaps a grand procession will emerge as necessary in order to move the group into church without losing ritual continuity. And this, in turn, will challenge the musicians' creativity. Other consequences will follow.

The important point I wish to make in all of this is that first things should come first. Primary symbols should be experienced as primary and secondary elements not allowed to overshadow what is more important. (How often have you been to an Easter vigil where the majority of the assembly had no opportunity whatsoever to feel or see any water, apart from a few folks on the aisle who received a sprinkle or two?) Liturgical planning happens best when first things come first.

In talking to groups around the country about ways to enrich their liturgical celebrations, I often say the sort of things written above. A common reaction is, "Yes, but. . ." and then a variety of reasons why it just isn't practical to do things the "right" way. Most often, the excuses have to do with limitations of time and energy and money. As a pastor myself, I recognize the realistic limitations under which we all labor. But my response is that we should at least pick a few things to do well, or at least better, each time we do a planning process. The alternative is to resign oneself to a generalized mediocrity that is self-perpetuating.

I have used the example of developing the primary symbols of the Easter vigil. Could not most communities approach their planning for Holy Week with a resolve to do the same for each of the major liturgies of the Triduum? It is fairly obvious that on Holy Thursday we need to look at how fully we symbolize a supper where tasty bread and cups of wine are shared by all. Jesus himself gave the symbolic link between the table experience and his sacrifice when he stooped to wash the disciples' feet. That, too, is a symbolic action deserving of considerable reflection, creative planning, and generous amounts of hard work to develop the choreography of the rite. Most communities know by now that Good Friday calls us to simplicity as the word is proclaimed, the cross venerated, and Communion shared. But little creative energy is generally directed at recapturing the vital symbol of wood, instrument of salvation. We still weaken our symbols by multiplying them, and the proliferation of crucifixes (not crosses) further confuses by shifting focus from the wood to the corpus as object of veneration. Perhaps we should sing (and translate?) *Ecce lignum crucis* seven times before planning that segment of the rite.

First things first. I have been making a case for a practical approach to liturgical planning and suggesting Holy Week's liturgies as an ideal place to try out this approach. It works all year round, for any celebration, but the Paschal liturgies provide us with particularly strong and evident symbols with which to begin. The proposal has the added advantage of being able to accommodate the planning mechanisms and resources of any community, regardless of size or circumstance. All it requires is that one not get lost in detail and lose the balance or flow of the various symbols that constitute our liturgical repertoire. Furthermore, this approach respects a fundamental principle of good liturgy in that it recognizes the connection between meaningful celebration and symbols that are allowed to speak with the expressive power that is natural to them.

THE POWER OF THE PROCESSION

Its power is underestimated, its potential untapped, its execution nearly always left to chance. I am speaking of the procession, one of the least appreciated aspects of liturgical experience today. Such neglect is astonishing in light of the venerable status enjoyed by this ancient feature of the liturgical repertoire. Not only liturgists, but other experts – those in the field of ritual studies or the dramatic arts, cultural anthropologists, and so forth – point out how important the procession is as a feature of religious ceremonials. I hope to heighten your awareness of the procession's importance and suggest ways parish liturgy teams might improve the quality of these ritual movements.

Stylized movement is a fundamental part of human "meaning-making." Virtually every culture has developed

symbolic meanings for the choreography of its various processions. The American tradition of parades, for example, is
still effective, as our recent experience with welcoming home
soldiers from the Persian Gulf has shown so forcefully. Many
a wedding reception still reaches its peak of celebratory fervor
when formality barriers break down enough for participants
to join in a group dance, which is often a form of serpentine
procession.

The Roman liturgical tradition is rich in its variety of
processional forms. During ancient stational liturgies in Je-
rusalem, Rome, and Byzantium, throngs of the faithful prayed
with their bodies as they moved from one sacred shrine to
another. Those processions have proven decisive in shaping
some of today's most important festal expressions. Hispanic
and African-American liturgies are often rich in processional
forms. Symbolic minimalism, however, which tends to afflict
current worship experience, has muted the sacred voice of
processions.

Both contemporary culture and ancient tradition illus-
trate how important it is for us to realize the potential of
religious processions if we are to vivify parish worship.

THE PARISH TAKES A LONG LOOK

Parish liturgy teams are well advised to assign a special task
force or subcommittee the job of studying and strategizing
how best to accomplish this challenging goal with the local
community. A year-long period of reflection, discussion,
planning, and experimentation would surely bear rich fruit.
The following suggestions are intended to stimulate the imaginations of parish teams and encourage them to invest the
effort needed to rediscover processions – one of the primary
liturgical symbols with which we worship God.

Start by brainstorming all the processions that might
conceivably be included in a parish's liturgical life. Members
will probably be surprised at how quickly a substantial list

can be generated. At every Sunday Eucharist, there are five processions (entrance, gospel, gifts, Communion, recessional). Every baptismal liturgy calls for a procession to the font. The order of Christian initiation of adults makes use of processions on numerous occasions (for example, in the rite of acceptance and at the election). Lent and the Triduum are filled with processions, from the approach to receive ashes to Palm Sunday, from Holy Thursday's eucharistic procession to Good Friday's veneration of the cross, and, of course, there is the elaborate choreography demanded at the Easter vigil, with its movements around fire, word, font, and table. Our devotional life is rich with processions, particularly in many ethnic groups that make up our parishes. Some parishes might have a May procession. Nearly every parish has the stations of the cross and eucharistic devotions with processional elements. The liturgy team could look at virtually every liturgical event in parish life, from the wedding procession to the solemn entrance of the casket at a funeral.

ASKING QUESTIONS

Once an exhaustive list has been generated, the group can categorize and analyze it from a variety of perspectives in order to understand all the factors at play. Which processions call for a limited number of participants and which should ideally involve everyone present in the actual movement? Which processions begin outdoors and move indoors, or vice versa, and which take place exclusively inside or outside? Which have a single destination and which have multiple stops? Which processions are meant to carry something (or someone) from one place to another, and which are meant for display purposes only, ending up where they started? What about the order of the participants? Who carries what and in which sequence? What functional categories might be used to group various kinds of processions, and what sort of "messages" are embodied in each? What are the roles of silence, music, rhythm? How is stylized movement and the interaction of various persons within the procession accomplished (that is, how is "dance" used)?

This analysis needs eventually to be informed by a growing understanding of the liturgical tradition, including the origins and meanings of various processions. Over time and through discussion, the group will develop a sensitivity to the nuances that are possible (and called for) within many different liturgical processions. Members will recognize the importance of the principle of progressive solemnity and will gradually develop a "feel" for the dynamics of ritual embodiment. They will become more astute observers of much that they had long taken for granted, and their observations will become important pieces of data as the group tries to get an accurate reading of the parish's experience over time.

CREATIVITY TAKES TIME

A wise group will not begin problem-solving too early. It will not rush to "fix" anything or be hasty in proposing change. Rather, members will give themselves generous amounts of time and space to reflect on and digest many a discussion without immediate practical consequences. They will explore, without definitive resolution, what various processions mean and all of the ways their meanings might be enhanced and expressed. They will discover that every authentic symbol is so layered with meanings as to be literally inexhaustible. There will be plenty of room for the creative process to ferment. The group will come to realize that any effort to deepen a parish's faith by renewing its experience of processions will have to range far and wide if it is ever to effect substantive change. Everything is connected – especially at liturgy – and the group will open many a can of worms as they discover how every liturgical symbol needs to be "opened up" if a community is to celebrate its faith at liturgy in ways that are vibrant and life-transforming.

The time will come, however, when the group will recognize that it must begin to act on its accumulated insights. Group members will have come to appreciate how provocative it is to engage worshipers on a bodily level. But they will not shrink from moving an entire Sunday morning assembly outside to welcome those who seek entrance into the catechumenate. They will learn the musical "tricks" that make processions work (repetitive phrasing, rhythmic patterns, coordination of sound amplification systems, and so forth). They will learn how to stage relaxed processions that are meant to be fun (yes, sometimes liturgy is meant to be fun!), and they will know how to create solemnity, precision, and grace. They will not be afraid (well, perhaps a little) to offer their presiders a lesson from the local drama coach on how to walk. And they will put enormous energy into how best to engage the assembly's imagination, touch its heart, and put a skip or two into its feet. They will try candlelight processions to rally parishioners for human rights or unborn life. They will attempt to revive the ancient experience of invoking the saints as they march to places of baptismal birth, and they will know when to let the assembly participate just by watching attentively, something most Americans learn early in life on the Fourth of July.

THE RESULT

The result of all these efforts will be a growing sense of unity and purpose among the assembly at worship. The assembly itself will come to know – because of what it experiences – that its members share a deep unity as the Body of Christ. Their identity as a pilgrim people will be shaped in powerful ways, and parish members will come to act out of that knowledge in surprising fashion. Processions are all about movement, change, and transformation. At a deep albeit subliminal level, the members of a community that learns to express itself through effective liturgical processions comes to know the importance of conversion, discipleship, and the following of Jesus.

INCENSE: THE DANCE OF THE HOLY SMOKE

For some people the use of incense at a liturgical celebration is a sign of the Tridentine Mass mentality and a sure indicator that those who favor it are stuck in a rigid conservatism. For others, incense is a symbol of New Age exotica that brings to mind hippies smoking pot in the sixties and all the bad things one might imagine about the liberal Left. I argue that using incense means neither of these, and that we would do well to retrieve its judicious use as a depoliticized but very important liturgical symbol.

THE POWER OF THE SYMBOL

One of the reasons that the use of incense can evoke such diverse reactions is because of its power as a liturgical symbol. Liturgists have long argued for a fuller and richer use of liturgical symbols because of the inherent power they contain. Strong, primary symbols grab us at a gut level in a way that neatly logical reasoning can never do. Symbols are charged with an energy and a primal force that are rooted deep within the human psyche.

Incense surely qualifies as such a symbol. It assaults the senses both on the visual and olfactory level. The rising smoke, which releases its odor, twists and curls its way into our imaginations. The liturgical "dance of the holy smoke" triggers subliminal memories of childhood reveries, watching clouds form mysterious shapes on a sunny afternoon in mid-summer. It recalls campfires and family fireplaces, slender columns of smoke rising from birthday candles, and a hundred other forgotten memories. Our olfactory associations, proven scientifically to be among our most durable memory traces, are also keenly affective in nature. They tend to "layer" experiences that are recalled in ways that give a depth of meaning that literally cannot be put into words.

No wonder, then, that incense has for millennia been used in religious settings where the human family gathers to act out its most solemn and important rituals. Given the power of incense, liturgy planners would do well to consider carefully how incense might best be used as part of a community's repertoire of liturgical symbols.

WHEN SHOULD INCENSE BE USED?

A community wishing to be thoughtful about its use of liturgical symbols should reflect carefully on the variety of settings in which incense might be used. Catholics will most often be exposed to its use during the course of a eucharistic celebration. *The General Instruction on the Roman Missal* (#235) specifies five occasions on which incense can be used at any eucharistic celebration. The recently published "Ceremonial of Bishops" gives an even more elaborate treatment of incensation (#84-98) and refers to the wide variety of other liturgical contexts in which incense is appropriate. A parish's liturgical planners should draw up as exhaustive a list as possible, specifying all of the times when incense might be used in their community. Then, using the principle of "progressive solemnity" as a guide, they can discuss which of those settings seems to call for its use. Like any other symbol, the impact of incense can be lessened by overuse. This means that planners will also need to discuss frequency of use. Some kinds of celebrations (for example, benediction) may seem always to require its use; others (for example, liturgy of the hours) may only call for it on more solemn occasions.

HOW SHOULD INCENSE BE USED?

The ritual choreography involved in the use of incense is an issue that generally is given little or no consideration. Yet, it is a matter that is as complex as it is crucial. Priests, depending on the era in which they received their seminary formation, had varying amounts and kinds of instruction on how best to use incense in a ritual context. Some were given rigid, mechanical rules to be followed; others barely were exposed to how to swing a thurible. Lay liturgical ministers have usually had no instruction at all in the matter. It seems safe to say that most communities would do well to "start from scratch" in their consideration of how to choreograph its use in the spirit of our revised liturgical rites.

Once again, planners are well-advised to begin by considering all of the possibilities. In some settings the familiar swings of a traditional thurible are exactly what is called for. But there may be times when a much more effective use of the symbol is achieved by a stationary container holding burning charcoal on which are placed (by a graceful liturgical dancer?) the grains of incense. The movement of the one applying the incense is, in fact, a kind of liturgical dance, despite the reluctance of many to use such terms to describe what is occurring. The stylized gestures called for in the ritual books (bowing, swinging arms, specified steps and paths to be taken) certainly qualify as choreography. And, like any dance form, its execution needs rehearsal, critique, and repeated practice if it is to seem – in the moment of celebration – effortless and unself-consciously graceful.

Planners need to consider many aspects of the use of incense in order to achieve the appropriate choreography for each ritual occasion. For example, they need to ask what is the nature or meaning of the action that accompanies its use. On a festal occasion such as a Eucharist celebrating a parish's hundredth anniversary, a grand entrance procession may be led by a series of ministers swinging brightly decorated thuribles. The Greek custom of placing little bells on the thurible, thus involving the auditory senses as well, would seem ideal for such an occasion. This would be in stark contrast to the way the priest would administer incense as a way of reverencing the body during the funeral liturgy. Occasionally, incense might be used with such subtlety that it merely suggests a mood or serves as a kind of decorative backdrop. Other times, it could be a crucial way to focus on some essential action that needs to be carried forward with dignity, solemnity, or a heightened sense of power.

WHICH VESSELS ARE BEST?

Most parishes have an old thurible with varying shades of tarnish and more than a few dents from playful or overly zealous altar boys. Stationary dispensers are often recycled clay pots or cannibalized parts from unused liturgical vessels. Once the importance of incense as a liturgical symbol is recognized, it will be obvious that great care needs to be given both to the container for the incense and to the incense itself. It is not out of the question to suggest that several thuribles and a variety of containers should be chosen to reflect degrees of solemnity and varieties of liturgical contexts. Planners will also have to acquaint themselves with the rich variety of scents available. The olfactory "connoisseurs" in the community will need to be recruited for something equivalent to a "wine tasting" session, at which different scents are chosen for different uses.

Does it all have to be so complicated? Why do we have to make such a "big deal" about incense and get liturgy committees and planners involved in everything in such elaborate fashion? The answer, of course, to such reservations is that when we come before God at worship everything *is* important. Ours is an incarnational and a sacramental faith, which means we must take seriously whatever has to do with our embodied ways of worshiping. Grace flows into our lives, we believe, in privileged fashion through the sacramental symbols we use in our rituals. The more carefully and reverently we execute and engage those symbols, the more they "open us" to the gift of grace enacted in our midst. Incense was called "holy smoke" for good reason; it puts us in touch with the Holy One in ways that are as elusive and transcendent as the sweet puffs that dance heavenward with our prayers.

FINDING GOD IN SILENT SPACES

Even the most convinced proponents of Vatican II's liturgical renewal concede that the old Latin liturgy was striking in its ability to create an aura of hushed prayer in the presence of hundreds of worshipers. The deep stillness of that quiet has created indelible memories for worshipers, who speak of experiencing a sacred presence, the palpable nearness of God. The silence that filled the assembly of believers as the priest whispered his prayers at the altar and the congregation fingered their beads or gently flipped the pages of their prayer books had been for many Catholics a profoundly religious moment of encounter with the divine.

It is understandable that with the changed forms of worship since Vatican II, many people express strong yearning for a return to such prayerful quiet. The participatory model of the reformed rites, it would seem, affords little opportunity for extended moments of deep prayer. Yet the documents of the renewal express a vision in which holy silence is a crucial part of liturgical experience.

REFLECTING ON CORPORATE SILENCE

The rubrics are discreet but clear; frequently they provide for "spaces" that are to be filled with prayerful quiet. Liturgy planners ought to reflect on the silences within the liturgy, planning ways to restore the practice of (and retrieve the positive values of) corporate silence, which was so strongly a part of pre-Vatican II tradition.

While the reformed rites of Vatican II are often blamed for the loss of prayerful quiet, such accusations are simplistic and unhelpful. Actually, cultural and social factors – as much as any liturgical changes – are responsible. One cannot underestimate, for example, the negative influence the mass media have had on our capacity for quiet. Television has conditioned us to consider both visual and auditory over-stimulation as normal. Strollers who carry "boom boxes," joggers with radio earphones, programmed Muzak in public spaces – all are symptomatic of a society no longer at ease with "the sound of silence." Conversely, the media's nonstop barrage of "sound bites" is the logical outcome of a culture that has forgotten how to reflect in silence on an idea worth pondering.

The current cultural aversion to quiet is no cause for discouragement or excuse for lament. Rather, highlighting it can remind liturgy planners that they have an extra task: preparing the assembly to enter with ease into an experience of silence that will be prayer-full. We can no longer presume that worshipers know how to enter and abide in the quiet. We need to help children learn the art of resting in silence; we must help their elders recover contemplative skills often long unused.

LEARNING THE ART OF SILENCE

The great religions of the world have always recognized prayer as a skill that must be taught. We need to devise ways to teach worshiping Catholics, young and old, how to use corporate silence as a way into prayerful encounter with God. Such instruction will have to be deliberate and explicit, without apology for setting aside time, whether as part of a religious education curriculum or as a prelude to Sunday

Eucharist. Techniques such as breathing exercises or physical relaxation may smack of Oriental mysticism to some, but they may be necessary for Westerners who wish to slow down their inner rhythms enough to rest in God's presence without worrying about "what comes next."

EVALUATE PARISH RITUALS

Liturgy planners are the most likely group in a parish to lobby for training the community in the art of silence. As a preliminary step, liturgy planners will need to assess the community's rituals to determine whether (and how well) they enable or prevent prayerful silence. Specifically, liturgical ministers (presiders, lectors, and cantors, for example) will need to pause long enough at the appropriate places for deep quiet to unfold within the assembly. It is not simply a matter of suggesting they count to fifty before moving on with a prayer, reading, or song.

Liturgical ministers must develop a feel for pausing "long enough but not too long," lest restlessness overtake the assembly. In addition, they will have to work together to extend gradually the assembly's "tolerance" for quiet. After a particularly powerful reading, for example, a cantor may want to double the "normal" time spent in quiet before beginning the psalm response; on another occasion, the group's restlessness or a poor reading may limit the quiet to a much shorter period of time. Parish ministers must develop the art of "reading an assembly" to determine its capacity for quiet in a given celebration, and liturgy planners can help them.

Ministers may also need to be shown the "tricks" that lead an assembly into quiet.

Short, carefully focused introductions to prayer, if spoken with proper inflection and pacing can bring an assembly gently but quickly to a moment of prayerful quiet.

The posture, muscle tension, and general carriage of the minister's body is also a powerful signal to the assembly. Such body language expresses whether the moment is one of just "waiting to get on to the next thing" or is actually a moment of brief but powerful stillness.

Eye contact, dealing with distractions, and placement of hands are all part of the way a minister signals to the assembly that it is time for quiet prayer.

If possible, videotape a liturgical celebration and then focus on the signals each minister gives the congregation. Such an exercise will profit any liturgy planning team wishing to improve its corporate silences.

DEVELOP A PLAN OF ACTION

A liturgy team deciding to make better silence a priority for the community will benefit by developing an overall plan of action. Rather than expanding simultaneously every feasible quiet time (for example, after all of the introductions to prayer, the readings, the homily, and Communion), the team agrees on a few priorities.

The team would consider how best to use – or not use – music during the collection and preparation of the gifts and after Communion, to name just two specific times. They would decide how to minimize distractions and how to promote quiet prayer at those times. In short, the liturgy team will need to look at every aspect of the situation in order to help the community develop a long-range strategy to restore corporate silence as an important element of liturgical prayer.

When the team is ready, it should apprise the rest of the community of its strategy and rationale. The team can then invite parishioners to join the effort, prayerfully using the times targeted for substantial silence.

These remarks are not a criticism of the reformed rites of Vatican II; the failure has not been in the rites, but in our neglect of all that they call us to do at prayer. In our enthusiasm for the "full and active participation" which is the "aim to be considered before all else" (CSL, #14), we liturgists may have forgotten how intense participatory worship can be when an assembly is lost in deep, quiet prayer. The challenge before us now is to go back to the reformed rites and rediscover where and how they invite us to silence.

BODY LANGUAGE IN THE LITURGY: WHAT IS IT SAYING?

Scene one: An episcopal liturgy in a very "high church" cathedral in the northeastern United States, where spit-and-polish seminarians are trained as acolytes with all the precision of the Marine Guard at Arlington's Tomb of the Unknown Soldier. With ramrod-straight posture, impassive countenance, and flawless bows, their bodies communicate eloquently a very particular notion of liturgical propriety.

Scene two: A parish church not far from the cathedral where the kindly old pastor recruits his acolytes each week from whomever happens to have arrived a few minutes early for Mass. On this particular occasion the pick of the day includes Billy, a distracted ten-year-old boy, who looks like "Pigpen" from the Peanuts comic strip, accompanied by his friend, Earl, who spent last night at Billy's house, but happens to be Jewish. The nonchalance of the former is matched by the bewilderment of the latter, and any suggestion of symmetry in their bodily actions is an example of the possibilities inherent in purely random movement.

In these examples, both the bishop and the pastor are pleased with the body language of their respective liturgical assistants. Neither is mindful of the bias about the nature of "good liturgy" that informs their preference for such different styles. Perhaps neither has ever given sustained thought during their years of presiding at liturgy to the impact of liturgical body language on the faith experience of those who gather for worship. Yet, inherent in those two radically different liturgical choreographies are alternative visions of church, sacrament, and worship. In fact, liturgical theologians might even want to press the case that on a deeper level what is being manifested are different understandings of God or, at least, different understandings of our relationship with God.

It could be argued, of course, that this is pretty heavy baggage to put on so peripheral an item as body language; after all, aren't these simply rubrical details? Or, in most cases, don't they involve stylistic features so unimportant that they are not even worth including in the rubrics? Yet I hope those who prepare parish liturgies are keenly aware of how truly important it is to give careful consideration to matters such as body language.

EVALUATING YOUR PARISH BODY LANGUAGE

Thoughtful liturgy planners would be well-advised to devote time and energy to an assessment of the body language that characterizes their parish liturgical celebrations. They could generate a list of all those who are part of the liturgical action from the presider to the acolyte and from the choir to the assembly at large. They would then identify and categorize basic issues such as posture change, movement from point to point, use of hands, bowing, genuflections, and so forth. Next they would have to tackle the more complex variables of style, speed, aesthetic balance, interactive dynamics with other elements of the liturgical action, and any other factors that contribute to the overall shape of the celebration.

Such an assessment would inevitably raise foundational questions about the nature of liturgy, about the respective roles of those involved in the celebration, as well as other theological and ecclesiological values implicit in the choreography of the ritual. Certainly, liturgical planners could also identify skills that need developing, changes of style required

---

in order to be more consistent with sound liturgical practice, and numerous other facets of body language that merit attention. Strategies could then be generated to deal with whatever has been selected for improvement or change.

POSTURE DURING THE EUCHARISTIC PRAYER

What concerns might emerge from such a close look at liturgical body language? One of the most dramatic examples of body language tied to faith-expression is the current practice of directing the assembly to kneel after the Holy until the Great Amen. As an act of eucharistic piety, the practice is usually justified by relating it to belief in the Real Presence. Unfortunately, it disrupts the unity of the eucharistic prayer (which begins at the preface dialogue), by requiring an abrupt change of posture that has little to justify its occurrence at that point. It also ignores one of the most ancient and evocative ways of professing faith in the Resurrection: standing erect for our most solemn moments of communal prayer. Further, it ignores the very text of the prayer that it accompanies, which refers to those present who "stand in your presence and serve you." Not surprisingly, many communities who thoughtfully examine the issue decide to remedy the situation by assuming a single posture (standing) throughout the entire eucharistic prayer.

LESSONS IN THE LANGUAGE OF THE BODY

Training for specific liturgical ministries often includes some measure of concern for body language. Workshops for presiders are usually quite sensitive to such matters. Usually, however, other liturgical ministers receive only scant training in how to use their bodies effectively for their roles. Liturgical planners who take seriously the concerns being raised here will want to review their procedures for training liturgical ministers. Do song leaders know how to use their arms well to gesture for the assembly's sung response? Do ministers of bread and cup serve with the aplomb of a four-star restaurant or the dispatch of a fast-food joint? Do acolytes shuffle, race, stumble, or prance? move with an unobtrusive grace and dignity? Do ushers lounge against the back wall like construction workers on their lunch hour? How does the assembly bow, cross themselves, genuflect, and so forth?

Some liturgy planners might want body language to occur "naturally," by which they mean without rehearsal and, they might suggest, without "pretense." Such a suggestion overlooks the fact that all ritual movements are learned behaviors; none is "natural" in the sense of being unrehearsed. Simply because we are oblivious to what we have learned and how it comes across does not make it more "natural" or appropriate. Rather, like anything we truly value and care about, body language at worship can communicate more effectively and gracefully if its movements are made with attention, thoughtfulness, and practiced ease.

FOSTERING PARTICIPATION

Many communities are learning the power of introducing the assembly to a fuller and more deliberate use of body language that can foster active participation in wonderful ways.

In communities where hearing impaired parishioners are present, the entire assembly can sign the words to the psalm refrain or other acclamations while they are being sung, adding a new dimension of awareness for everyone.

While the presider says a blessing over catechumens or others who seek special prayer, the whole assembly can join the body language, extending their hands as an expression of their solidarity with the presider's prayer.

On Good Friday at the veneration of the cross, bows or other gestures can accompany the community's song in ways that are tremendously expressive and deeply prayerful.

At the Sunday renewal of baptism, those present might be invited to take water from a common bowl and sign one another's forehead with a cross.

Such efforts in leading the assembly into a more generous use of body language at prayer will, of course, have to be made thoughtfully and introduced with sensitivity. Like all of the symbols we use at liturgy, our body language must be marked by authenticity, simplicity, and dignity. The dialogue among liturgy planners who seek to discern what is most appropriate for their community can be rich and fruitful on many levels.

FILLING OUT YOUR PARISH ART
AND ENVIRONMENT REPORT CARD

We live at a time in history when Catholics seem particularly insensitive to the importance of the environment and aesthetics of the spaces in which they worship. The United States bishops' document *Environment and Art in Catholic Worship* notwithstanding, in most parish churches there seems to be little concern for or pursuit of "the beautiful" as an essential ingredient of liturgical celebrations. In fact, it is probably the generally poor state of affairs in this regard that prompted the U.S. bishops to issue that important document in the first place.

I write to encourage parish liturgy teams to do a kind of "audit" – or, perhaps, examination of conscience is the better term – in the area of environment and art.

Most of us who are concerned about things liturgical have our antennae up when we visit other churches. We notice how others organize their rituals, we compare their choirs and music selection to our own, we check out their pamphlet racks and browse through their bulletins for new ideas. We are struck by the clutter in the vestibule, and we marvel at the extraordinarily tawdry art work that graces their niches.

But, sadly, those same antennae unconsciously seem to retract when we return home. We are so accustomed to our own environment that it takes a special, deliberate effort to notice even the most basic things that would immediately strike a visitor.

LOOK AGAIN, AS IF FOR THE FIRST TIME

Imagine the benefit if we could keep those antennae up as we visit our own parish church, as if for the first time! In fact, such an opportunity exists, if only we take the time and effort to do so. The primary suggestion of this article is that the parish liturgy team gather on a crisp fall afternoon for an "audit" of the environment and aesthetics which unconsciously shape parishioners' experience of worship all year round.

Spend an hour or two helping one another observe things as if you were seeing them for the first time. Take copious notes. Record impressions. Pretend you have never before seen the place where this community gathers to worship, and let the physical impressions of the place speak to you of the values and vision which define the identity of your parish.

After the tour, members of the liturgy team should spend time reflecting on their experience and on what they observed. The team will also want to reread *Environment and Art in Catholic Worship* in light of their observations. And then, in most parishes, they will want to begin a conversation that will certainly raise some challenging and provocative questions. These questions, if faced squarely, will lead to decisions that will have significant consequences in most parish churches.

How might such an "audit" proceed and what might be some of its consequences?

ENVIRONMENTAL AUDIT: STEP ONE

Once in the parking lot (or, in an urban setting, once assembled on the sidewalk), look around and observe what you see. What are the "first impressions" that a visitor would receive? What strikes the eye and speaks most powerfully of the identity of this community? Are there signs? Are they legible? Do they compete with one another or other focal points? Undoubtedly, in some parishes, the "message" intended or not, will be that this is a place where BINGO is the most important thing happening. Or the message may be that the people who live here don't believe in maintaining the appearance of their buildings (grounds, paint, etc.). Or, a more positive message may be given. The team should linger outside long enough to take in all the information there is to collect. Long-neglected maintenance needs will suddenly become evident, aesthetic judgments of a previous generation may be called into question, practical issues like traffic flow or handicapped accessibility may be raised, and so forth.

STEP TWO

Enter the building, again with the eyes and ears of one arriving in this space for the very first time. Church vestibules are fascinating places. Someday a great book will be written describing how one can analyze the personality of a parish just by visiting its vestibule, much as a skilled therapist can look deeply into the psyche of a client by careful observation of body language.

In ancient Rome, there was such a sharply defined need for a proper "transitional space" that basilicas were often built with great courtyards through which one had to pass before entering the interior of the church building. The flowing fountains and lush vegetation in the courtyard were meant to be evocative of the garden of paradise, and they were highly successful in serving their purpose of providing a "buffer zone" from worldly distractions. It is a rare church vestibule today that would lay claim to such a function. But whether intentional or not, the transitional space of a building does shape the readiness for worship of those who make the passage from outside to inside. The liturgy team will want to scrutinize carefully how the vestibule works upon those who enter. Aside from noting that some of the posters are years out of date, consideration might be given to color, wall covering, lighting, floor texture, and obstacles impeding the traffic flow.

STEP THREE

Pass through the vestibule into the main worship space. The team should linger a bit just inside to receive the full impact of the "first impression" this space makes on a visitor. That gestalt will be fleeting, but especially important, because it will often capture the dominant elements that shape the experience of worshipers – albeit unconsciously – throughout the year.

Is the experience one of a dark and ponderous space? a space that is light and uplifting? a place of clutter and distractions? a place with a single focal point to which the eye is immediately drawn? a repository of great beauty? an inviting place welcoming the pilgrim? a foul and dank place in need of cleaning? a reverberant space of lively echoes that invites song, or a space deadened with heavy carpeting and cushioned seats? Answering these questions will require being in touch with feelings that may be transitory and hard to identify. But the effort is worthwhile, because the resulting awareness among team members can be highly instructive as the team later tries to identify and prioritize the agenda which results from its audit.

STEP FOUR

Once the whole impression of the worship space has been absorbed, the group should begin to move about and focus on specific elements. The limits of this brief article preclude any attempt to list the full scope of what ought to be examined. The major furnishings and the basic elements that shape the environment will, of course, be given careful attention. These will be obvious and need not be enumerated here.

The team should take stock of less obvious elements as well. Artistic detailing never before noticed, paint that is peeling on the ceiling, lights that are not properly focused, cracks in the stained glass windows, wrinkled, cheap looking banners that seemed so beautiful five years ago. These and many, many other aspects of the space should be seen and noted. Team members should wander about, taking in all that their senses can absorb, and they should record carefully for later discussion and reflection their feelings and thoughts about what they are experiencing. After team members have had ample time to make their observations on their own, they might profit from some time pointing out to each other what they observe, helping one another to sharpen their powers of observation by seeing with others' eyes.

USING THE OBSERVATIONS

The members of the liturgy team should have in mind a clear plan about how they will proceed once their on-site visit is completed. Before they gather to discuss results, they may want parish members with specialized skills to examine particular aspects of the worship space. Perhaps there is a landscaper in the parish who could submit an evaluation of the grounds; perhaps an architect would love to have a chance at last to comment professionally on her own church; perhaps there are artists or painting contractors or lighting specialists. In other words, the team should invite others with particular competencies to submit their respective observations.

Once the entire observation phase has been completed, the team should begin a strategic planning process. That will involve evaluation of the data in light of *Environment and Art in Catholic Worship* as well as other relevant liturgical documents and aesthetic principles. After evaluation will come a priority list of identified needs, then an action plan to address immediate concerns, as well as a longer range plan to secure funds or take other steps in order to address all of the needs that have been identified.

Imagine where a community could be twenty-five years from now if one of its identified needs is the creation of a special fund to commission first-rate works of art for its place of worship! Some sort of mechanism should also be put in place to provide for ongoing attention to aesthetic and environmental issues. It might take the form of scheduling an annual audit such as the one just completed, the establishment of a permanent group to attend to these matters, or other strategies that better fit the local scene.

APPRECIATING BEAUTY

The process of recovering in our Catholic population an appreciation for the importance of beauty in our places of worship will be a gradual and long-term one. However, such a recovery is a vital element in the overall project of liturgical reform and renewal mandated by Vatican II. Our ancestors in the recent and distant past have left us eloquent testimony to the value they put upon places of worship that proclaimed to the world a God of goodness, truth, and beauty. Our generation must now take on the challenge of that tradition and speak to the women and men of our time in buildings that rise above the ugly shabbiness that has become so commonplace in recent generations.

THE CENTRALITY OF MUSIC IN WORSHIP

Recently, I was interviewed by a priest who was preparing to accept a pastorate after many years in administrative/diocesan office ministries. He wanted to take the pulse of

parochial life and get a better sense of the pastoral priorities
in parishes today. At one point, he posed a very probing
question: "If you were in a parish with very limited financial
resources and multiple needs, where first would you spend
your money?" I gave the question serious thought before
answering, "I'd invest in getting the best possible musical
resources for the weekend liturgies."

My answer was self-revelatory in that it showed me
something I had never before put in so stark a fashion. It has
to do with a strongly held conviction of mine about the
absolutely crucial importance of music in creating a vibrant
liturgical celebration. Only music can create, sustain, and
express the depth of meaning we seek to capture in celebratory
moments of great significance.

Consider the images that filled television screens when
Nelson Mandela was inaugurated: hundreds of thousands of
people were caught up in a transcendent moment, where only
with the music of their liberation anthem could they hope
to capture the meaning of the historic events unfolding
around them. It is inconceivable that such an occasion would
have been marked without music, or with the insipid song
that characterizes Sunday worship in many American parishes.

Of course, one need not point to such epochal events
as the end of apartheid to realize how essential music is for
authentic celebration. How many parishioners who appear
musically mute on Sunday morning would refrain from singing enthusiastically when their four-year-old's cake is brought
in blazing with birthday candles? Even so, we still have not
truly grasped that music is intrinsic to the idiom of liturgical
celebration. Too often, music is treated as an "extra" that
adds solemnity and festivity, rather than being the very way
we worship. Even in parishes where music has a firm place
at Sunday celebrations, its role may be seen as secondary and

peripheral, not really having a claim on our first attention
and best energies.

FIVE MUSICAL KEYS

To help me understand the basic issues at stake regarding
parish music, I asked several pastoral musicians in touch with
the musical scene around the country what the neuralgic
points are that "make the difference" in determining the
quality of a parish's liturgical music program. Then I reread
Music in Catholic Worship (1972, 1983) from the Bishops'
Committee on the Liturgy, and the more recent and very
important report from the Milwaukee Symposia for Church
Composers (1992) reviewed in the Summer 1993 issue of
Church. After digesting the wisdom of these sources and
reflecting on my own experience, I have identified several
key areas which, it seems to me, a parish's liturgical leaders
must take into careful consideration.

- *Musicians must be formed in good liturgical practice.* Parish musicians have a real responsibility to exercise leadership within the community. It is unfair to them, and
  certainly to the community, to ask them to do so if
  they are not well grounded in the basics of good liturgy.
  Not every parish needs to have a musician with aca-
  demic credentials in liturgy. But every musician who
  exercises liturgical leadership needs to have more than
  a casual acquaintance with liturgical theory.
  Many dioceses have resources and/or a regular program
  of formation for parish musicians. For those that do
  not, musicians will need to educate themselves through
  conferences, workshops, seminars, and guided study.
  Most of all, those responsible for the parish's liturgical
  life – including the musicians themselves – need to see
  ongoing formation as a high priority deserving of appropriate support in the form of budget allocations and
  time to participate in formation events. No matter how

skilled a musician may be in the musical arts, if there is not a solid understanding of the demands of the liturgical tradition, that musicianship will too often miss the mark and result in poor celebration.

- *A community must avail itself of high-quality musical resources.* A major reason some parish music programs limp is limited commitment – financial and otherwise – to procure high- quality resources. Some parishes offer only a missalette; others provide multiple hymnals or print their own worship guides weekly to allow for an extended repertoire. It is a question of priorities.

  While some parishes enhance their sound system and the acoustical properties of their worship space to pro-mote better singing, others are satisfied with crackling amplifiers and wheezing speakers that absorb so much sound that Pavarotti would have difficulty filling the room with song. It is a question of priorities. Some parishes have excellent piano, organ, wind instruments, brass, strings, handbells, and synthesizers; others be-grudge the cost of an annual piano tuning or resist periodic repairs to the pipe organ as long as it is partially operational.

  Some parishes have "developed" bad taste by cultivating liturgical music of poor quality; others have refined their sensibilities and developed an ear for what is of enduring value. Some parishes supply the assembly with song leaders and an instrumentalist at every liturgy; others have a "choir Mass" and let the remaining cele-brations get by with a poorly trained folk group or nothing at all.

- *The entire assembly must participate fully in the musical experience.* My father's side of the family was about as musical as a large stone, and my father was no exception. But I can't remember a single birthday party for us kids where he didn't join the rest of us in a chorus of "Happy

Birthday." It was important to him that we all joined in the singing. The example is a simple one, but it holds true when the parish family gathers around the eucharistic table.

Parishes need to foster the attitude that everyone's participation is essential to the community's worship. The formation required to accomplish this will take generations, to be sure, but few liturgical needs are as crucial. All in the assembly must feel their responsibility for the success of the community's prayer and must see their own involvement in the community's song as integral to it.

For that to happen, a range of issues must be dealt with sensitively. The idiom or style of music must be within the cultural universe of those present. Liturgical musicians must employ deliberate strategies in selecting music that can be mastered by the assembly. Also, there must be a sustained effort to form and support the assembly's voice as it grows into its musical role. No musician would expect a choir to show up on a Sunday morning and to sing its first note during the opening song. All singers need to rehearse a bit to warm up their voices and to make sure they remember the music. Similarly, at every celebration where the assembly sings, there ought to be a warm-up beforehand and, when needed, some teaching to make sure the worshipers have mastered the repertoire.

* *The community needs a core musical repertoire.* Many parishioners of good will are kept from participating fully in the music at worship because they are not familiar with the repertoire. (See "100 Songs Every Parish Should Sing" by Sheila Browne and Richard M. Gibala in the Summer 1994 issue of *Church.*)

Only a small part of the general population can pick up new music quickly and sing along with ease. Given unmusical genes, I sympathize with all who have to work at learning a new piece of music before it becomes familiar enough to sing comfortably. Since Catholics are relatively young in experiencing the vernacular liturgy, it is little wonder that we are still at the early stages of developing a basic repertoire.

Although musicians want to stay abreast of new developments in liturgical music, they must remember that most assemblies need to go much more slowly in absorbing new music than does the professional musician. Many parishes still lack a unified vision of what to include in and how to develop a common musical repertoire for the entire community. In such parishes, each Mass has its own style and repertoire, and rarely the twain do meet!

A better idea is for the parish musical leaders to plan carefully what will constitute its core repertoire and strategize carefully how best to make certain that everyone in the assembly learns it and is comfortable singing it. This is not an argument against diversity of styles within a single parish. Rather, it is a reminder that amid the diversity there also needs to be a thoughtfully developed core of music. Then all can participate, especially when special feasts call for the gathering of the entire community.

- *Musical selection follows function.* In other words, the function music plays within the overall liturgical action determines which musical piece ought to be used. All too often, musical choices are made for a variety of secondary reasons, with little or no attention given to the demands of the ritual action itself. Although a particular song may fit well with the theme the homilist plans to emphasize, it should not be used as an opening song unless it serves well in gathering the assembly. Certain parts of the liturgical action call for acclamatory music, for example, which requires a particular sort of musical choice. Responsorial psalmody has a very specific function within the liturgy of the word, and selecting the proper text and music on a given occasion requires a feel for that specificity.

Our liturgical tradition is rich in its ritual components, nearly all of which have an appropriate musical literature that respects the integrity of each. Those who select the parish music must understand how each ritual component fits with the others in the celebration. For example, when a procession is called for, certain kinds of music would simply be inappropriate. If the action is consecratory gesture accompanied by acclamation from the people, then a specific kind of musical response is called for. Communities ought to avoid falling into patterns of selecting familiar music without regard for the specific musical demands of the ritual action. The issue highlights the need for musicians to be formed in good liturgical practice.

IV.

CELEBRATING THE
TIMES OF OUR LIVES

WEDDINGS

Too often since the promulgation of the rite of marriage,
liturgical planning for the celebration has consisted of the
parish priest's handing the engaged couple a copy of Joseph
Champlin's *Together for Life* and giving them the phone
number of the parish organist. If they choose readings and
prayers thoughtfully, and select music without a major battle
over pop tunes, everyone considers the process a success.

Perhaps we have reached a sufficient level of maturity
in the liturgical renewal to recognize how much this falls
short of the ideal. Many of the principles of good liturgy,
which by now have become commonplace in our Sunday
celebrations, are still little in evidence when it comes to the
wedding liturgy. It may be useful to point to a few of those
principles and to some of the more obvious ways that a parish
might work on its wedding liturgies to bring them more into
line with the renewal achieved in other liturgical contexts.

FULL AND ACTIVE PARTICIPATION

This foundational principle which the *Constitution on the
Sacred Liturgy* says is "the aim to be considered before all

else" (CSL, #14) is sadly neglected in the celebration of most wedding liturgies. By and large, weddings are still passive spectator events for all but the wedding party. The presence of the unchurched and of worshipers from many different congregations at a wedding makes this neglect understandable, but nonetheless deplorable. First things first, then: everyone involved in a parish's wedding liturgies needs to be clear about this primary goal and work to accomplish it.

Music is not meant to be just pleasing background filler; it is one of the most important ways the assembly actively participates in the celebration. In most cases, this will mean a parish policy that establishes a song leader as the norm for every celebration. More than just a performing soloist, the song leader is one who helps the assembly understand its active role as well as learn its assigned music. This will entail such essentials as wedding programs that give the assembly a copy of the music for their parts and ample but not protracted rehearsal time once everyone is assembled. A gathering hymn after the entrance procession gives the assembly an immediate sense of their active role; responsorial psalms that are quickly learned and easily sung are available in abundance these days; eucharistic acclamations using the "echo" technique makes participation accessible to all. Even with all of this congregational song, there are still many opportunities for soloist recitals during prelude, postlude, offertory, and Communion.

CREATIVE ADAPTATION

We are mostly beyond the stage of thinking that a reading from Gibran's *The Prophet* is the ultimate in creative adaptation, but there still seems to be too much gimmickry in many attempts to personalize the wedding liturgy. What is needed is an approach to adaptation that recognizes what good liturgy looks like and aims to enhance the ceremony along those lines. For example, the old attitude that a wedding "is the bride's day" produces a public display of private piety, such as her trip to the Madonna statue to lay a rose. On the other hand, good liturgical understanding that sacraments are celebrations of the church, not exercises in private piety, will seek to develop that insight, for example, by putting the nuptial blessing to music with acclamations for the assembly interspersed. Keener liturgical sensitivities will result in bridal couples who face the assembly to exchange vows in audible tones, instead of showing the assembly their backs as they whisper "I do" at a presider's promptings. The two official witnesses also might better express their role by offering testimony to the assembly about the couple's readiness and seriousness of intent, rather than merging with the sea of onlookers who passively observe what the couple is about. These are just a few examples of adaptations that are much more in tune with principles of good liturgical celebration than some of our more currently popular additions, such as the "candle" ceremony. But how, one might ask, can we expect to steer couples away from maudlin sentiment and turn them in this direction?

A GOOD PLANNING PROCESS

Good liturgical planning does not happen spontaneously. Parishes have a responsibility to help couples – most of whom have little experience in this area – to come to good judgments about how to shape their wedding celebration. This will require some careful thought and strategizing by the "professionals" of the parish, in order to develop uncomplicated structures and marshal helpful resources for the couple to use. The book *Celebrating Marriage,* reviewed in the Spring 1989 issue of *Church* (p. 44), is one of the best written sources available. Parishes will probably do well to elaborate their own list of options for the couple to consider, and to make sure that there is someone available to sit down and help them understand the advantages of doing things certain ways. Many parish musicians have put together cassette tapes of music best suited for various points in the liturgy. The idea works equally well in explaining other options that the couple may wish to consider. Explanations of how liturgical symbols function in the celebration can be most enlightening and helpful to the couple who may never have reflected on that topic before. The insights available, for example, in *Environment and Art in Catholic Worship*, regarding the strength of primary symbols and the weakness of secondary symbols, could easily help a couple avoid some of the common pitfalls.

LITURGICAL PLANNING MUST PARALLEL SPIRITUAL FORMATION

Marriage preparation programs in place today are far superior to what was available ten or twenty years ago. A host of topics are well treated from the dynamics of relationships, to the impact of financial stress on family life, to sophisticated approaches to understanding the functioning of family systems. Perhaps one area that has not always kept pace in this rapidly improving preparation process is the area of faith formation. Yet, it is almost axiomatic that good liturgical celebrations emerge from mature faith experience. Our theology of marriage is still woefully underdeveloped compared to other areas of sacramental catechesis. We still do not do a good job at helping couples reflect on how their life experience is connected to the rituals of marriage. We still are not very adept at helping them reflect on personal meaning and then connect that with the story of Jesus as it has been lived and celebrated in our tradition right down to the present moment of their own wedding liturgy. This remains a task to be accomplished in ever better and more skillful ways. The spiritual formation that is called for as part of our marriage preparation program will be along these lines; and, if we are successful in imparting it, couples will surely plan liturgies that are more realistic, as well as more mature.

KEEP THE FOCUS WHERE IT BELONGS

We mentioned above the commonplace attitude that the wedding is "the bride's day." That piece of popular wisdom is only one of the cultural traps we face in trying to celebrate marriage within a thoroughly Christian context. We need to help couples and the families in our parishes reflect more critically on what our culture considers appropriate in celebrating weddings. Someone needs to proclaim the good news that we do not have to engage in lavish display or conspicuous consumerism in order to show the quality of our love or our sense of God's presence in our relationships. Remembrance of the poor and the needy even in planning a wedding seems entirely appropriate and even fitting. If marriage is one of the sacraments of Christian vocation, then the bride and groom, whatever their social and economic situation, need to direct a good deal of energy to defining their sense of mission in the world as a couple, and how best to express that commitment in the celebration. The real challenge of liturgical planning is to stir such thoughts, not only in the hearts of the bride and groom, but in all who participate in the rite that begins the couple's married union.

THE ORDER OF CHRISTIAN FUNERALS

The recently issued *Order of Christian Funerals* is gradually making its way onto bookshelves in sacristies, rectories, and other places where liturgical practitioners ply their trade. In some parishes, the arrival of the new Order will cause barely a ripple of change; in others, it will occasion a genuine renewal of the entire way a community ministers to its members at the time of death. How ought a parish to act, so that its response to the new Order falls in the latter category, not the former? The reflections that follow may help to answer that question.

For more than twenty years now, new ritual books spawned by the directives in the *Constitution on the Sacred Liturgy* have been published, one after another. Understandably, the edge of excitement has lessened somewhat as successive editions of the "renewed" liturgical rites arrive. But it is a tragedy amounting to betrayal if we take those new texts and merely put them in the old wineskins of familiar routine, instead of recognizing the call to renewal which they represent.

THE DIFFERENCE BETWEEN PROMULGATION AND RECEPTION

Professional liturgists recognize the distinction between the promulgation of a new text and its reception. Promulgation is a simple matter of church law, a date that is set to begin using the new text, usually accompanied by an official decree forbidding continued use of the previous ritual. But reception of a liturgical text is a gradual, ongoing process – a phenomenon that is more the work of the Spirit than of ecclesiastical decree makers. Reception usually takes years and even generations, as the vision and spirit of a new liturgical rite is gradually assimilated into the fabric of Christian life and experience. Promulgation of the *Order of Christian Funerals* now offers parishes the opportunity to begin work on the task of its reception.

THE NEW *ORDER OF CHRISTIAN FUNERALS*

Like many of the reformed rites, the new *Order of Christian Funerals* does not contain anything so dramatically different as to force parishes to deal with it in a totally new way. Its "newness" and its renewing power are more subtle and even rather easily missed. What is required, in order to catch its renewed spirit, is a careful study of the entire text, especially the introductions found throughout the volume. One of the most characteristic features of the revised rites of Vatican II is the importance of the pastoral introductions, which give not only rubrical details but also the basic theological vision out of which one must operate in order to celebrate the rituals properly. Often the directives about ecclesial ministries which these introductions provide are as significant as anything else in the document. This is certainly the case with the new *Order of Christian Funerals.*

INTEGRATING PASTORAL CARE AND RITUAL CELEBRATION

The new Order assumes a context of pastoral care at the time of death in which many different ministries will be involved. The progression of specific "moments" for which rituals are offered requires a variety of pastoral care ministers who can deal effectively with the needs of those who mourn. The sections of the Order entitled "Prayers after Death," "Gathering in the Presence of the Body," and "Transfer of the Body," all contain rites which will require very specific sensitivities in order to be celebrated well. Frequently, those who lead these celebrations will be someone other than the parish priest. This means that parishes that strive to implement the full vision of the new Order will need to spend time helping those pastoral ministers learn some of the basic skills required to preside over and adapt appropriately the rituals provided. So clearly linked are pastoral care and ritual celebration in the Order, that the two are virtually inseparable. The "new consciousness" which this integrative vision reflects will surely constitute one of the greatest challenges a parish faces as it implements the new Order.

One final word needs to be added about the wealth of new texts which are provided in the Order. Careful, thoughtful selection of the most appropriate textual options is an extremely important element in a proper celebration of the rites. There are so many texts now available for all of the variable parts that considerable time will be required to familiarize ourselves with all of the options.

THE REASON FOR OUR HOPE

In a society where the denial of death is still one of our most anti-Christian cultural forces, communities once again are called upon to hold up the reason for our hope and why it is we celebrate in the midst of grief and loss. Anthropologists remind us that how a society buries its dead is one of the most telling indicators of cultural value. Parishes have the opportunity with the *Order of Christian Funerals* to reexamine, renew, and revitalize some of the core issues that bind us together as believers. When one reads carefully the texts in the Order, it quickly becomes clear that pastoral care at the time of death is meant to be only one aspect of how parish ministers reach out to people in times of crisis and loss.

The way the new Order treats each individual situation according to its unique demands is a model of pastoral sensitivity and flexibility. The rich variety of new prayers in the volume and the constant reminders to adapt to every situation speak powerfully to the way liturgical celebration must flow from the real-life experience of those who gather to worship. Those who would still do every funeral much the same way, with well-worn phrases of a stock funeral homily and the same three hymns sung at every Mass, will find little support in the Order.

What is most exciting about the potential of the new rite is that it expects so much of those who use it. *The Order of Christian Funerals,* because it touches so vital a nerve in our human experience, offers a specially powerful force for renewal of personal and communal faith.

A (RE)NEW(ED) LOOK AT THE RITES AND SYMBOLS

One of the opportunities offered by the publication of the Order is its invitation to look anew at the ritual symbols we use to celebrate a Christian's passage to God at death. Although there are no major changes in the ritual structure, which by now has become familiar to us, several issues relating to rites and symbols merit a fresh look. The use of water, incense, Easter candle, pall, and other Christian symbols must be carefully considered. The options built into the rite demand that decisions for their use be based on sound liturgical and pastoral judgments, not just routine or habit.

One element of the final commendation that is often overlooked is particularly worthy of reflection. The Order suggests that the song of farewell is to be the "climax" of the rite of final commendation. Although it is permitted to substitute spoken invocations when music is impossible, this song is suggested as one of the places where "preference should be given to the singing." Current practice in the United States shows widespread neglect of the ritual potential of this climactic song. Parishes need to discover ways to make the singing of the song of farewell a powerful communal experience which will "affirm hope and trust in the Paschal mystery" as the rite intends. Where satisfactory musical settings for the texts provided cannot be found, the rite allows the selection of any appropriate song.

One other element worth reconsideration is contained in the rite of committal. Although it is not required, the Order clearly assumes that the body will be committed to the earth as part of the ritual action. If the committal does not take place during the course of the rite itself, then it is to be done "at the conclusion" (but still, clearly, as part) of the ritual action. This certainly runs head-on against our American denial of death, which is reflected in the use of mortuary chapels rather than graveside committals, or the custom of lowering the body into the earth only after the mourners have departed. One hopes the prophetic voice of the Order in this regard will encourage more and more parishes to opt for the ritual act of committal as an important way of coming to grips with the finality of death. It is a painful time to be sure, but in the long run much healthier than the other ways our culture tries to shield us from the reality of death.

COMMUNAL ANOINTING

Many of the changes ushered in by the liturgical reform of Vatican II were a source of distress for some and confusion for others. Few changes were as universally acclaimed and readily accepted as the council's decision to refurbish the sacrament of anointing as one of healing rather than dying. What was once perceived as the church's "kiss of death," has been rediscovered as a source of new hope and strength for countless believers. But for all of the positive gains that have been made thus far in the reform of this sacrament, one suspects that much yet remains that might open up even further benefits for those who celebrate well the rites of anointing. What follows are some ideas that may serve as reminders or suggestions to help in assessing whether a community is achieving the full potential of this sacrament.

PASTORAL CARE

The title given the ritual book (*Pastoral Care of the Sick*) contains a powerful clue to one of the most crucial features in the reform of anointing: pastoral care. It makes sense to see and celebrate the fact that a community's care for those in their midst who suffer must be broad. Where parishes have taken seriously the rite's call to pastoral care, new ministries have flourished in response to the full range of human needs experienced by the ailing. Where pastoral care infrastructures have been neglected, celebrations more often than not reveal the inadequacy of a community's ritual rather than its power for healing. In a parish where eucharistic ministers regularly take Communion to the sick and homebound, where caregivers attend to the material and social needs of their suffering brothers and sisters, where the sick are held up and revered as witnesses to the cross of Christ, in such parishes the celebration of anointing rings with a truth that none can mistake.

COMMUNITY

By now it is a truism to observe that the communal form of the sacrament is the "preferred" form in which it is to be celebrated. Even in emergency or extreme circumstances, the rite asks the presider to gather with him a small number of believers who will represent the larger community of faith. Happily, celebration of the sacrament in its communal form is becoming a regular feature of parish life across our nation. Indeed, in a parish where communal celebrations are not provided, one might well ask whether the leadership of the parish is fulfilling its pastoral responsibility as it ought.

The rite's simplicity easily lends itself to inclusion in even the Sunday eucharistic celebration. But whatever judgment is made about the best time to schedule the communal form of the sacrament, the assembly itself is of primary importance in the celebration. Every effort needs to be made to highlight the fact that it is the community gathered that is the source of prayer for healing. The presider is not the shaman who alone has the words that restore; he is the one who gives voice to the prayer of the assembly, which, as the Body of Christ, can always count on its prayer being heard. Each parish will have to decide how best to express this ownership of the rite, but it seems essential to make special provisions for the active participation of the community in ways that are noticeable and striking.

TOUCH

Liturgists stress constantly the need to let primary symbols in the sacraments "speak" in a way that is not overcome by secondary elements of the rite. The symbol of touch is surely one of the most primary, expressive symbols in this rite of caring and healing. In the loving touch of Christ the healer, we are connected to primordial powers that echo across cultures and down through the centuries. Who of us cannot remember what a mother's touch meant at times when we were sick? In this rite, the laying on of hands by the presider must be done with all of the solemnity and deliberateness possible. The silence that is called for at this time ought not to be overlaid with "filler music," as if the silence of the moment were not full enough. When hands are laid on a bowed head, and allowed to rest there tenderly, as deep prayer is said over the one who is sick, an entire community can be riveted in empathetic solidarity and called to prayer in a way that words could never achieve. Many communities have also discovered how powerful it can be to have the presider invite members of the assembly to join him in laying on hands. The remarks above concerning the community's involvement can also be strongly implemented by such an invitation.

OIL

At the risk of belaboring the obvious, we must also point out the centrality of the oil used for the anointing in order for the celebration to reach its full potential. It is a sad fact that in too many communities still today, the oil of anointing is never seen by the community or the sick person. What is seen is a tiny holder with greased cotton, and only on very close inspection do forehead or palms reveal traces of sacred balm. What ought to happen, instead, is for the assembly and the sick person to be shown a graceful, crystal container filled with an abundance of precious, soothing oil. And the oil ought not to remain a mere object of admiration. It must be experienced. That is, its application should be generous enough for all to see and experience – until echoes are heard of the gospel scene in which oil was lavished on the Lord as a sign of love. It is not just oil that is the sign of the sacrament, but oil applied to forehead, palms, and wherever else needs healing. A presider's dainty concern with delicate application in most cases does more than anything else to quench the spirit of this rich ritual gesture.

PRAYER

Once again we point to an element in the rite that is so obvious as to appear to need little comment. Yet, it is at the heart of the matter. The Letter of James reminds us that "the prayer of faith" will save the sick person. In the ritual, we make that prayer throughout the celebration, but especially in the litany that precedes the anointing. Unfortunately, it is a prayer all too easily given only passing attention. But it is also ripe with possibilities for achieving that full, communal involvement mentioned above. Those possibilities can be achieved in many ways, for example, by a solemn, sung proclamation with communal response, and by intentions that are carefully crafted to reflect both this community's real concerns, as well as the universal longings that we tap into via this sacrament. Communal celebrations of anointing that "work" are invariably those in which the assembly has been drawn into a deep, authentic prayer through the words and gestures of the rite.

COMMUNION OF THE SICK

Many parishes view ministry to the sick and homebound primarily as a part of the community's pastoral outreach efforts, giving its liturgical dimensions little or no attention. Yet the book *Pastoral Care of the Sick*, which contains pastoral and liturgical directions for bringing Communion to the sick and homebound, is part of the Roman Ritual. As such it has as much claim on the attention of parish liturgy teams as does any other sacramental ritual. I offer here several reflections on the liturgical aspects of ministering to the sick.

THEOLOGICAL CONSIDERATIONS

The proper celebration of any liturgical ritual requires (1) a renewed theological understanding of the rite and (2) an understanding of what makes a healthy context of pastoral care. This is certainly the case with the ritual for offering Communion to the sick. The introduction to *Pastoral Care of the Sick* views the suffering of the sick in the light of Jesus' own Paschal mystery. Rather than seeing persons who are sick as objects of compassion and pity, the church regards them as valuable witnesses to the deep Christian meaning of suffering. As faithful witnesses to the suffering Christ, the sick are vital members of the church. For its part, the church's ministry to the sick is meant to reveal the face of the compassionate Christ. The patient attitude of those who are sick, in turn, reveals to the community the face of the obedient Christ, who accepted even suffering and death as the Father's will.

An understanding of the truth of this mutual ministry between the sick and their community is crucial if the sick are to assume an active role in the liturgical celebration of Communion, and not be passive recipients. As does every liturgy, Communion of the sick presumes an assembly of believers (even if they number only two), all of whom participate fully and actively according to their respective roles. Inviting the sick person to have a say in the selection of Scripture readings or in the formulation of intercessory prayers is not just a nice thing to do. The active involvement of the sick in preparing and celebrating the ritual, even in modest ways, expresses an important theological conviction: that the sick person is above all a believer, an active agent in the celebration, a vital part of the community of faith whose gathering gives fitting worship and praise to God.

A final theological consideration is the profound unity that exists between the sick person and the rest of the community, despite the isolation sickness tends to impose on the one who is ill. In Communion, literally, the bond of unity is both realized and celebrated. As the ritual states (PCS, #73): "The links between the community's eucharistic celebration, especially on the Lord's Day, and the Communion of the sick are intimate and manifold." For this reason, the ritual suggests that Communion be brought to the sick from the community's Sunday eucharistic celebration because "this symbol of unity . . . has the deepest significance on the Lord's Day."

LITURGICAL CONSIDERATIONS

Those responsible for the parish's liturgical life will want to spend some time assessing how Communion of the sick is currently being celebrated and to make determinations about where and how improvements might be made. This will undoubtedly involve collaboration and some training with those providing both pastoral care and the liturgical ministry for the sick. The following are some of the areas that merit attention:

Preparing the Space

The ritual suggests that some preparation of the place where the sick will receive Communion is in order. It specifically mentions a table dressed with linen, candles, and holy water. As with all other aspects of the celebration, enormous latitude is needed in order to accommodate the unique aspects of each situation. But what should be common to all is that attention and care be given to preparing an environment that is both prayerful and beautiful. There is no mention of fresh flowers, but what a wonderful sign of life they are to those who are ill! Obviously, the demands of attending to the environment ought not to be experienced as a burden either by the sick person or by caregivers. However, some discussion of what is possible and appropriate seems warranted by the pastoral minister as a way of expressing the importance of this sacramental gathering. The container(s) in which the minister carries the eucharistic element(s) to the sick should also live up to the standards of beauty and authenticity expressed in the document *Environment and Art in Catholic Worship.* Many households will lack the artistic eye or the resourcefulness needed to prepare the space appropriately. It would be a wonderful expression of the community's concern if someone on the liturgy team were available to help with this.

Preparing and Adapting the Ritual

The needs of the one who is ill will determine in every case how elaborate or how minimal the ritual should be. Great pastoral sensitivity is needed, but so is a high degree of liturgical sensitivity if the preparation and adaptation are to be done appropriately. We have already mentioned the desirability of involving the sick person in the planning of the celebration in some meaningful way. Although in many cases it will not be feasible, it should always be done where it seems practical. The minister should have a grasp of the essential structure of the rite, what its important elements are, and how it may be adapted in a variety of situations.

The introductory rites (greeting, sprinkling, penitential) are meant to prepare those gathered for worship. How much or how little should be done is at the discretion of the minister. There could be situations in which singing a gathering song is appropriate. Or, at the other end of the spectrum, a simple sign of the cross might be all that seems manageable. The liturgy of the word (reading, response, intercessions) must show a similar flexibility. In order to maintain a link with the Sunday assembly, one or more readings from that celebration might well be proclaimed, together with a report on the homily. Remember, with the sick, less is often more, and a single brief passage well proclaimed can be highly effective. The principle of distribution of roles in liturgical celebrations suggests that it is preferable for someone other than the presider to proclaim the scriptural text (as well as the intercessions) if there is such a person present. A brief homily is recommended whenever possible, applying the readings to the situation of the sick person.

The liturgy of Holy Communion (Lord's Prayer, Communion, silent prayer, prayer after Communion) although brief is the heart of this liturgy. The ritual foresees the possibility that Communion may routinely be provided under both kinds. In cases of necessity it also provides for sharing only the Precious Blood. Pastoral Care of the Sick also has another section for use when the sick person is dying. In that event, Communion is given as Viaticum, and the ritual may include renewal of one's baptismal promises, a litany, sign of peace, and the special words which accompany the offering of the sacrament (preferably under both kinds). Ministers who regularly take Communion to the sick and homebound will probably need some special preparation in order to become comfortable with how and when to use the ritual for Viaticum. The concluding rite is suitably brief, containing only a closing blessing.

PASTORAL CONSIDERATIONS

In order to insure a proper liturgical celebration of Communion of the sick, certain pastoral considerations are in order. Taking into account the condition of the sick person is, of course, the first priority. The minister needs to exercise great sensitivity and flexibility to guarantee that this is always kept in mind. Also, because this celebration is an act of public worship as well as being a service for the sick, a communal setting is always preferred. Most often this will include caregivers and immediate family, and, from time to time, there may be opportunities for expanding the circle of involvement.

The ritual for Communion of the sick is only one part of what is contained in *Pastoral Care of the Sick*. In addition, there is material for simple visits to the sick, visits to a sick child, anointing, and a variety of resources for the dying. Those who preside at Communion of the sick should be familiar with the other rituals the sick may need on occasion. Whether it be the sacrament of penance, anointing, or other prayers and ministries of the community, the Communion minister frequently is the first to recognize such needs and the one in the best position to make the appropriate referral.

A final question concerns the appropriate frequency for celebrating Communion of the sick. Naturally, the needs of each individual will determine the answer to the question. The ritual indicates that the sick have a right to "receive the Eucharist frequently, even daily" (PCS, #72). To secure this level of pastoral care, most communities would require a fully developed lay ministry.

Illness sometimes affords the sick a great opportunity for spiritual growth. Skilled pastoral care ministers will help the sick to center that growth in a solid eucharistic piety. Communion of the sick should be seen as a ministry of spiritual formation, as well as one of healing and nurture. It is not unusual for a person to develop a significantly deeper appreciation for the Eucharist during a serious illness. And, as their appreciation grows, so may their hunger for the Eucharist and their requests to receive Communion with greater frequency.

THE DAILY PRAYER OF THE CHURCH

In the grand scheme of liturgical renewal mandated by the *Constitution on the Sacred Liturgy*, an entire chapter was devoted to the reform of the Divine Office, the daily prayer of the church. The General Instruction of the Liturgy of the Hours, which accompanied the revised books of the office when they were eventually published, numbered the public and common prayer of God's people "among the primary duties of the church." Clearly, it was the council's aim to restore to the church at large the vast treasury of prayer embodied in the liturgy of the hours.

Perhaps it is premature to call this part of the general liturgical reform a failure. But it is by now unmistakably clear that we have not flocked in great numbers to reclaim daily prayer as our own. Over time, daily prayer has become almost exclusively associated with the clergy and religious. Some would have us admit defeat and give up. More true to the hope that is within us, it seems, is a patient and realistic approach which continues the effort to restore to God's people the prayer that is their birthright. What follows are some suggestions as to how we might work toward that end.

PREPARE THE SOIL

We cannot expect to change overnight a situation that has endured for centuries. If God's people are to enter into a regular experience of the liturgy of the hours as their daily prayer, then we must lay the groundwork in several ways. First of all, our people need to be much more knowledgeable about the Scriptures than is presently the case. The psalms, in particular, must be familiar friends whose passions, laments, and cries of praise have become second nature to us. We have before us a work of introduction and explanation that will need to go on for some time to come. Second, we need to help people to develop habits of corporate prayer in which they come to experience the truth that they, not just a priest-presider, are "doing" the prayer. The assembly must experience itself regularly as the subject of prayer rather than as mere spectators, in order for those habits to settle comfortably into hearts and souls. Finally, we need to restore to people a sense of the liturgical action as a corporate "duty" of the church – the act of a people who cannot not gather for praise of God. The ancient notion that the liturgy is the "people's work" must eventually replace our consumer mentality that has people participate in worship for the good feelings it produces rather than because they "owe" God such homage. The attitude sought here, of course, is not mere compliance with an externally imposed duty, but internal assent to a responsibility we feel to the very tips of our toes.

Preparing the soil of people's minds and hearts in this way is obviously not going to be easy or quickly accomplished. Yet, if there is ever to be a real return to the hours as a deeply felt daily prayer of the church, then we have no other choice.

UNDERSTAND THE PRAYER

Many of the efforts put forth by pastoral leaders in recent years to encourage a wider use of the liturgy of the hours have faltered because of a failure to understand the nature of the prayer itself. Despite its versatility and built-in flexibility, the liturgy of the hours does have an integrity of its own and cannot survive an infinite number of metamorphoses. Its structure, rhythms, and aims must be respected. There are numerous popular sources available today to help leaders attain a deeper appreciation for what the hours is and what it is not. Pastoral workers, liturgy committee members, and others interested in revitalizing the prayer life of their community can readily find appropriate materials to read and study that will help them to avoid many of the pitfalls of a sincere but uninformed attempt to restore the hours. As is often the case, clarity about a few basic points can be of enormous help. It is a prayer attuned to the rhythm of the days and the seasons. It is a communal prayer. Its hallmark is the notion of praise. The psalms – poems set to music –

are the cornerstone. Grasp well these basics, and you will not stray too far.

LOOK FOR THE RIGHT OPPORTUNITIES

Not too long ago Catholic life was a richly quilted fabric of novenas and devotions that could serve people's prayer needs in various settings at home and in the larger community. Scholars have noted that the development of those prayer forms was connected to the people's loss of an active role in understanding and participating in the "official" liturgical prayers of the church. With the restoration of the vernacular and the historic reforms of the eucharistic liturgy, there occurred a dramatic replacement of those "popular" prayers with the celebration of the Eucharist. The wave of "home masses" in the early seventies was the first sign of a growing tendency to celebrate virtually every occasion with a Eucharist rather than look at other prayer possibilities. The task and challenge we face now is to identify and reclaim those situations where the church's daily prayer would be the more appropriate form of liturgical celebration. We need also to identify and develop those opportunities where some form of the hours can replace hastily mumbled prayers that open or close parish meetings. Catechetical gatherings for children, retreats for youth and adults, vacation Bible schools, catechumenal sessions, major parish occasions of all sorts – these are the kinds of situations that require close examination to see if the hours might be the most appropriate way to celebrate the faith that draws us together.

GIVE THEM WHAT THEY NEED

One of the major obstacles that many have encountered in their efforts to restore the hours for more general use has been the lack of proper resources to enable people to pray the hours easily. Nothing can guarantee discouragement more than giving people one of the massive volumes of the hours that contains more material than they could ever begin to manage. How often has a parish celebration of the hours been just an exercise in page-turning and fumbling with song sheets and hymnals, rather than true prayer? Less is more, here as elsewhere. That means we need to make it extremely simple for people to pray the hours. We need to provide them with everything they require to participate in the prayer effortlessly and without confusion. Song must be accessible, easily learned and shared. Cues must be clear, leadership of the celebration sure and strong. The rich proliferation of music for the responsorial psalms on Sunday has in fact taught our people many ways and texts that allow them to enter easily into the experience of sung psalmody. Often just a cantor, even without accompaniment, can make for a beautiful and prayerful experience of the hours. We need always to remember that in the hours we ought not to strive for novelty and elaborate effect. The comfortable and the familiar, melodies and prayers used often enough to become a part of our very being – these are the ingredients for "success" in celebrating the hours.

USE OPTIONS CREATIVELY

The multivolume collection published by Rome as the reformed liturgy of the hours contains an elaborate repertoire of prayer and is a remarkable synthesis of centuries of tradition. But it is not meant to be followed slavishly at every level of the Christian family. What may become effortless routine in a monastic community can seem overwhelmingly complex to the less sophisticated. We need to approach the official version of the hours as a sourcebook that offers structure, models, and materials, to be adapted freely according to local needs. This adaptation, of course, must flow from a proper understanding of the nature of the hours as mentioned above. But adapt we must, if we are to help God's people pray the hours in ways that are natural and authentic.

The mention of creativity in liturgical planning often conjures up images of gimmickry and artifice. We must be clear that the creativity intended here has nothing to do with such superficial efforts. Rather, shaping a prayer experience by using forms that will move people more deeply into the silence of God is the truly creative task we propose. Sometimes it takes more creativity to attain simplicity than to pile on frills that merely distract. What is required is the ability to step back from routine and see the familiar in new ways. Rather than inventing new ritual forms, creative liturgical planning takes the accustomed and is able to breathe into it new life and vitality.

BE PERSISTENT

We need to recognize that the work of restoring the liturgy of the hours to God's people is a task that will span many generations. There is no quick fix that will offer shortcuts. Patient, persistent efforts will be required to introduce people to the hours, to help them learn its grammar and syntax, to lead them to attain fluency and even eloquence. We will be able to measure progress, if at all, only over a period of years. The fruits of our labors will be tiny mustard seeds at first, and only much later a larger growth. But for those who are convinced that such prayer is among "the primary duties of the church," we have no choice but to work tirelessly to give back to God's people their daily prayer.

PREPARING FOR ADVENT

The Fathers of Vatican II taught that the annual liturgical cycle of feasts and seasons "unfolds the whole mystery of Christ" in such a way that it allows us to experience his presence in our midst, deepening our encounter with the mysteries of redemption and God's saving grace (CSL, #102).

Such a vision is lofty, indeed. Its realization challenges parish liturgy teams working to turn such conciliar rhetoric into reality.

The goal is that the mysteries of salvation, unfolded throughout the liturgical cycle, will decisively shape the experience of believers, influencing their consciousness, their values, and their behavior. For a secular analogy, consider the way in which Super Bowl Sunday has, in recent years, shaped the ethos of American society. Many Americans literally arrange their lives around that ritual, which affects their consciousness and forms (to some degree, as well as reflects) their values. The vision of liturgical renewal is that Christian consciousness is similarly formed by the unfolding of the annual cycle of feasts and seasons enshrined in the liturgical calendar.

Sometimes, of course, the sacred and secular calendars, as well as values, conflict. I can think of no more formidable challenge in this regard than the church's efforts to reclaim the liturgical season of Advent from the forces of consumerism and commercialism. Advent regularly competes with a frenzied period of marketing, ritualized with secular symbols. Christmas is anticipated so early (before Thanksgiving!) as to eclipse totally any hint of Advent waiting or preparation. Any parish liturgy team that thinks its "countercultural" efforts to reclaim Advent will meet with easy victory is in desperate need of reality therapy. Nonetheless, the liturgy team unwilling to engage in the struggle is not worth its salt.

How might a responsible parish liturgy team go about the business of preparing for the liturgical season of Advent? What should be the scope of its efforts, and how might it proceed?

FOCUSING THE LITURGY TEAM

The starting point of the team's work should be a process of study and reflection. The nature of the Advent season is somewhat complex, resulting as it does from a historical evolution that is also rather complicated. Fortunately, there are a number of popular commentaries on the liturgical seasons available that make this part of the work relatively easy. The team needs to understand at least how Advent intertwines eschatological themes (which focus on Christ's coming at the end of time) with incarnational themes (which focus on Christ's coming in human flesh). The process of study should involve a careful reading both of the assigned Scriptures (including the weekday lectionary) and of the texts found in the sacramentary and the liturgy of the hours. Once immersed in this "world" of liturgical readings, the team can reflect on the themes and emphases that seem to resonate most forcefully with the needs and experiences of their own particular parish community. That reflection, in turn, will allow them to make the practical decisions needed as part of an informed and intentional planning strategy.

As one might expect, the basic focus of the team will be the ritual celebrations that occur during the season. The Sunday Eucharist, of course, is primary in this regard. The decisions to be made include the customary issues – such as choice of music, which options to use among texts, any particular efforts to choreograph the ritual differently (through silence, processions, dance, etc.) – as well as additional elements such as the lighting of the Advent wreath or use of a Jesse tree.

In order to provide a cohesive experience of the entire season, the team will want to look broadly at all of the rituals that make up the repertoire of the community's worship during Advent. Consider solemn celebrations of the liturgy of the hours, weekday Masses, special children's celebrations, communal reconciliation, anointing of the sick, and devotions. In addition to regular ongoing devotions will there be other events such as Christmas pageants or caroling, special

Marian observances connected to the feast of the Immaculate Conception, or Saint Nicholas day events for the children?

The liturgy team needs to consider matters broadly so that parish life will have a proper rhythm and balance consistent with the vision developed during the study and reflection phase of its work. Advent in the parish can easily become cluttered with events of varying degrees of appropriateness, with no one in a position to oversee how all of the events work (or don't work) together. If the liturgy team is willing to assume this broader responsibility, it will inevitably find itself dealing with matters that are not, strictly speaking, liturgical. However, it seems fair to say that a narrow focus on ritual alone – one that ignores the broader pastoral context of the community's life – will result in only limited effectiveness.

COORDINATION AND COLLABORATION

Obviously, the liturgy team cannot and ought not take over the jobs of every other segment of parish life. But if we are serious about the rhythm of the liturgical cycle setting the rhythm of parish life, then extensive collaboration is required among all decision makers in the parish. The liturgy team will want to touch base, for example, with those shaping the social justice agenda for the parish.

What should be the context of appeals for volunteers to provide Christmas food baskets for the poor?

Is it possible to integrate a Christmas toy collection for the needy with a children's celebration of Saint Nicholas day?

Can the people who sell Christmas trees in the parking lot be offered music for their loudspeakers that is more appropriate than "Rudolph the Red-Nosed Reindeer"?

Are there some take-home materials for families that the Director of Religious Education can provide which are liturgically appropriate, reinforcing the efforts of the liturgy team?

Should there be special bulletin inserts offering "alternative Christmas" purchasing opportunities?

Once a team begins to look at the broad pastoral landscape of parishioners' lives, the forces at work and the coordination of efforts necessary may seem overwhelming. But, unless we are willing at least to begin moving in this direction, our liturgical celebrations will continue to be gloriously out of touch with the rest of the fabric of people's lives. Homilists may continue to rail against the commercialization of Christmas, but without an alternative that the community can offer in rich and practical detail, people will naturally follow their accustomed patterns.

When the liturgy team starts to move in the direction suggested here, they may anticipate the accusation that they are overstepping their bounds. In response, one can only hope that team members proceed by way of invitation and explanation rather than defensiveness or belligerence. The renewal suggested by Vatican II is a profound one, to be accomplished over many, many generations. What a privilege it is for liturgy teams to be in the early stages of such a momentous task! And where better to begin than at the beginning of our liturgical cycle.

V.

CHRISTIAN INITIATION

INFANT BAPTISM AT SUNDAY MASS

It is relatively easy to make a strong case for a parish community to celebrate infant baptism regularly during the Sunday Eucharist. Official documents clearly promote the values of this more fully communal form of welcoming new members into the community. Most parishes have tried it at some point along the way, but surprisingly few have made it a regular feature of their liturgical schedule. Explanations for this failure include parishioners' displeasure over the few extra minutes required of them, or parents' resistance, but these may well be convenient excuses masking the more decisive factor: For busy presiders and liturgists already trying to cope with the demands of Sunday morning, it just seems like too much to ask on a regular basis.

Careful preparation and attention to detail can help to overcome the logistical obstacles that can often seem so overwhelming on a Sunday morning. The work of preparation must still be done, but the pastoral benefits for a community that takes seriously the celebration of initiation have long since been proven. The checklist that follows can serve as a guide and help in organizing a smooth celebration of infant baptism during the Sunday Eucharist. It might also serve to raise some new possibilities and encourage better ways of using the ritual.

GREETERS

There should be a team of specially prepared welcomers to greet families and friends arriving for the baptism. Last-minute questions, name tags or flowers, reminders about where to go and what to do – all of these can be handled by greeters who have as their only concern a warm welcome and the desire to make everyone feel comfortable. Many communities use the couples who help in parent-preparation sessions in this role since they are already known to the new parents.

RESERVED SEATING

There should be a section marked off for family and friends so that even last-minute arrivals can be seated comfortably and easily. If parents have been asked beforehand how many seats to save for their party, the special greeters can handle this task with little difficulty.

ENTRANCE PROCESSION

Including parents, godparents, and infants in the entrance procession is a good way to signal the important role they play in the celebration. Here, too, the special greeters can offer valuable help in getting bottles and baby bags settled in their places beforehand, and then helping everyone assemble for the procession.

QUESTIONING PARENTS AND GODPARENTS

The questions put to the parents about what they seek of the church for their child offer an excellent opportunity to make the celebration more personal. Parents should be well prepared during preparation sessions and encouraged to answer this question in their own words. The presider should hand the microphone to the parents and step aside so they can directly address the assembly. Parental nervousness is no excuse for the minimalistic one-word answer ("Baptism/Faith") suggested in the rite. This is a major opportunity offered to parents who seek the church's help in sharing the Christian faith with their children, and they should make full use of it.

OPENING RITES

The custom of abbreviating the introductory rites whenever there is another ritual insertion seems like an advisable adaptation to make on this occasion. The penitential rites and Gloria might well be dropped, and the presider move directly from signing the infants to the opening prayer.

READINGS

Communities that regularly include baptisms as part of the Sunday Eucharist would probably not want to get into the habit of substituting the assigned lectionary readings with baptismal texts. Occasionally, however, there might be reasons to replace one of the readings with a passage more appropriate to the occasion.

HOMILY

It is a mistaken notion that the homilist must preach a special "baptismal homily" whenever there are infants being baptized. He may wish to do so on occasion, but just as often he may choose to stick to the readings of the day and the message they inspire. After the homily and a period of silence, suitable transitional remarks can shift the focus to the upcoming baptism.

CREED

It seems redundant to have the creed shortly before the profession of baptismal promises. Much more logical is the custom of inviting the assembly to join with parents and godparents in responding to each of the questions that form the rejection of evil/profession of faith.

LITANY OF SAINTS

This ritual element is ideally a full version of the litany, sung solemnly by cantor and assembly, as the procession moves to the baptistry. Most parish churches do not have the grand spaces that permit such solemn procession, and so the litany is correspondingly abbreviated. Some communities even find it helpful to join the litany in some way to the general intercessions, linking the saints' prayers to our own.

VISIBILITY

This is an important factor to consider in the celebration of baptism at Mass. The assembly should be seated to allow them to see more easily, and they should not have to crane their necks to follow the ceremony. This may mean doing the baptisms in the sanctuary rather than at a rear or side baptistry area.

IMMERSION

As a fuller and more expressive sign, baptism by immersion is the preferred form to be followed. Where the present baptistry may be inadequate, a baby's bassinet suitably draped can serve nicely. Hot water placed in the basin before Mass starts is properly warm by the time for baptisms. If parents are advised to bring their child to church clad only in diaper and warm blanket, the mechanics are easily managed. Immediately after immersion, each child is wrapped in a towel and taken to a nearby changing table. The time for drying and dressing is covered by a rousing baptismal song acclaimed by the assembly.

ANOINTING

Sacred chrism can be displayed in a fine crystal decanter or cruet for all to see. Enough should be used to allow all to experience its fragrant aroma as well as its loving application.

BAPTISMAL GARMENT

What sense does the tiny bib make that masquerades as a baptismal robe? Better to change the text of the prayer to refer to the white garments, which they wear already; or, better, have them ritually clothed in an actual baptismal robe after the anointing.

CANDLE

Many parishes supply baptismal candles. However, the conferral of the light of Christ can be significantly enriched when the candle has been made by the family or godparents, or even members of the local community. The baptismal candle should have substance and beauty that reflect the stature of the Paschal candle of which it is an echo.

GIFTS

During the preparation of the gifts, many parishes invite parents and godparents to take an active role. The celebration might on occasion have a more developed ritual involving clothing the altar, presentation of special gifts reflective of the occasion, and so forth.

All of the ideas listed above are meant to jog the imagination and serve as a practical reminder of what can easily be done to enhance a parish's celebration of infant initiation. Careful planning and thorough preparation are the essential ingredients for success in this, as in so many other liturgical celebrations.

Catechumenate for Children

When the National Conference of Catholic Bishops met in plenary session in November 1986, they approved adaptations of the Order of Christian Initiation of Adults for use in the United States and promulgated a series of national statutes governing its implementation. Since the effective date of those texts was mandated in 1988, parishes throughout our country have progressively awakened to the implications of fully implementing the vision articulated in the order.

Initially, most parishes focus solely on a catechumenate for adults. Soon afterward they begin to wrestle with the fact that the order also calls for a catechumenal experience for children of catechetical age who are undergoing initiation. Although some parishes have simply thrown up their hands in despair and opted to integrate such youngsters into the parish's ongoing religious education program, others have accepted the challenge of a distinctive initiatory process for children and are learning, with the children, just what that means for a parish.

RITUAL AND CHILDREN

The order envisions ritual experience as an integral component of the catechumenal formation process. In other words, without the benefit of a full and robust celebration of the rites of the catechumenate, an individual's conversion will be partial and incomplete. This fact is certainly as true of children as it is of adults. Therefore, parishes wishing to provide a catechumenate for children need to give careful consideration to the adequacy of the rituals with which children celebrate their progress throughout the initiation process.

This means that parish liturgy teams (as well as the catechumenal team) need to consider carefully how they celebrate the rite of acceptance (or welcome), the rites called for during the period of the catechumenate (anointing, minor exorcism, blessing, liturgies of the word, and perhaps the presentations), the rite of sending (or election), the scrutinies (or penitential rites), as well as the celebration of initiation itself at the vigil.

The following ideas will assist parishes in their efforts to celebrate in the best possible way these rites with children.

CHILDREN'S RITUAL WITHIN THE ASSEMBLY

In the section of the order dealing with children, there seems to be a strange reserve about celebrating catechumenal rituals in the midst of the community's full assemblies. This reticence is based on a concern that the children not be made to feel uncomfortable in the presence of a large group of adults. Extensive experience throughout our country has shown that this fear is quite unfounded. After some initial shyness, most children grow to love the attention that is showered upon them when they play a prominent role in the liturgical celebration.

The high value the Order places on celebrating initiation "within the community of the faithful" (*CSL*, 14) clearly ought to bias liturgy planners in that direction. Only under very specific circumstances and with good reason should the major rites of the catechumenate be celebrated apart from the normal assembly of the community.

CHILDREN AND ADULTS TOGETHER?

A second decision liturgy planners must make is whether or not to celebrate with both children and adults in the same ritual. There is no automatic answer. If there are a large number of adults and only one child, there may be legitimate concern about the child getting "lost" in a ritual. The same holds true for a single adult in a large group of children. On the other hand, a desire to keep the members of a family together might be an overriding concern favoring a joint celebration. The need to make special ritual adaptations to accommodate the developmental level of the children in question might at times favor a distinct celebration. Or, a community's wish to stress the fundamental reality that there is only one catechumenate in any parish, despite separate formation efforts for different age groupings, might dictate a joint celebration. Obviously, nothing should be decided without considering each specific case. The best decision will be reached when planners look carefully at all of the operative factors each time a ritual is to be celebrated.

LITURGICAL ADAPTATION

This brings us to our next consideration: the need for adaptation. One of the greatest benefits the order has brought to parishes is the realization that liturgical adaptation is not an optional activity. Once mistakenly considered the domain of liturgical "liberals," adaptation of official ritual is clearly mandated by the order. Simply to do the rite "from the book" would be to do the rite badly. There are too many elements that require thoughtful adaptation.

The need to adapt the rituals each time they are celebrated has forced planners to understand more deeply a whole host of issues:

- the structure and content of various rituals
- how to read the aesthetic as well as the religious needs of diverse cultural groups who gather to worship
- how to implement the principle of progressive solemnity.

Prepared or not, parish liturgy teams are faced with an imposing challenge to adapt complex rituals intelligently and faithfully to a changing variety of situations. Where planners have undertaken this task well, they invariably listen to both the demands of our liturgical tradition and to the experience of the participants who will engage in the ritual.

CHILDREN'S RELIGIOUS EXPERIENCE

The catechumenate for children has helped many to realize that children's religious experience is not a "watered-down" version of adult experience. Nor should the rituals that celebrate children's emerging faith be simple reductions of the adult catechumenal celebrations. The most thoughtful and skilled adaptations for children occur when liturgy planners are in close contact with the shape of the children's conversion experience. Authentic ritual is always engaging, for adults as well as children. As long as there is a sensitive interplay of the symbolic forms of the ritual with the real-life experience of the participants (adults or children), the danger of contrived, "kiddie" versions of catechumenal liturgies will be avoided.

CONCLUSION

If my remarks seem long on generalities and short on specifics, it is because I want to avoid contriving solutions to every possible parish situation. What is most important is that some basic premises be kept in perspective when planning the celebration of catechumenal liturgies for children. Communities that have taken seriously the need to celebrate fully and well the rites for children face substantial challenges and rewards.

We in the church are still at the beginning of our efforts to implement the Order, both for adults and children. What has already become clear, however, is that we must devote the same care and energy to celebrating initiation with children as we have begun to do with adults.

RCIA & LENTEN PLANNING: SOME PROPOSED CHANGES

At its annual meeting in November 1986, the NCCB approved the definitive "White Book" revision of the Rite of

Christian Initiation of Adults (RCIA) together with a series of newly developed rites for use in the dioceses of the United States. At the same time, the bishops also approved canonical statutes governing the catechumenate and set a mandatory date of February 2, 1988 (the First Sunday of Lent), for the implementation of the RCIA.

In addition to the liturgical rites it provides, the RCIA also envisions a process of pastoral care and formation which underlies and prepares for those celebrations. Many communities will require some time to develop that process fully, as is clear from the NCCB's decision to establish a five-year plan of implementation. But celebration of the rites is no longer optional and even in the absence of a developed catechumenate process, initiation of catechumens and candidates for reception into full communion must now be according to the norms contained in the RCIA.

RITE OF SENDING/ELECTION

One of the most striking contributions of the new book of rites is the way it has helped parishes to begin the Lenten season with the proper initiatory focus. In response to the many complaints from those who felt that the bishop's celebration of election in the cathedral detracted from a parish's efforts, there is now a parish Rite of Sending that preserves the values both of a diocesan-wide gathering and the local community's witness on behalf of the readiness of catechumens and candidates. The giving of testimony is clearly the high point of the parish rite, and planners will want to ensure that it is done properly. This means that sponsors and others who know them will tell of the conversion journeys that have prepared catechumens and candidates for full initiation during the Triduum. The testimony that is given should avoid two extremes: On the one hand, confidentiality must be respected and highly personal material ought never be disclosed in the public forum. On the other hand, triviality is also to be avoided, as are speeches that sound more like award banquets than the discernment of the Spirit in one's life. Others in the community will be invited to speak as well. Provisions must also be made so that all who speak are audible to the entire assembly. Most often, the ritual of signing the Book of the Elect will be the climax of the parish rite. That means a handsome book and a ritual choreography that is clearly sacred action, not mere formality.

Planners should also note that a children's Rite of Election has been created and may be appropriate for parishes with a developed process for children A further decision that must be made concerns how a parish will ritualize the different status of those elected for baptism and those who are candidates for reception into full communion. Now rites are provided for the already baptized who will use the Lenten season to complete their preparation, and a rite is offered for communities where both baptized and unbaptized are present at the same celebration. Local planners will have to determine which rite(s) seems most appropriate to use and then prepare the celebration with sensitivity to ecumenical concerns, as well as to the pastoral realities that reflect the participants' conversion-in-progress.

SCRUTINIES

The "White Book" contains a newly written scrutiny/penitential rite for the already baptized, which is to be used on the Second Sunday of Lent. The traditional rites of the Third, Fourth, and Fifth Sundays of Lent are reserved for the unbaptized. Here again planners will need to discern how best to celebrate these prayers of deliverance and strengthening, which are needed by baptized and unbaptized alike. Properly done, these rituals can be powerful moments in a community's Lenten conversion experience. They can speak to the multiple forms under which evil manifests itself in our day, and they can do so with the reassuring conviction that in

Jesus our victory over evil is assured. But that will only happen when they are prepared for and celebrated with a care that signals their importance and solemnity. These rites are not optional; to omit them requires a special dispensation from the local bishop and then only for grave reasons, such is their importance.

Meditation on the prayer texts and their accompanying readings (lectionary Cycle A is to be used) will reveal how radical is the mystery of evil with which we grapple in the scrutinies: In the first scrutiny, the figure of the woman at the well invites reflection on evil which is born of personal fault. Jesus confronts the Samaritan in all of us, asking that we accept responsibility for our history of sin and find in him reconciling forgiveness. In the second scrutiny, the figure of the man born blind invites reflection on social sin, the evil of the world into which we are born. Here too, we celebrate our discovery that Jesus is light in a sin-darkened world, that in him evils that are greater than we as individuals can be lifted. Finally, in scrutiny three, the figure of Lazarus becomes a metaphor for ultimate evil, sin which is unto death because it is a refusal of life itself. As Jesus calls Lazarus to life, candidates, elect and all in our community should have a powerful experience of what a scrutiny is all about. Effective planning of these scrutinies will be sobering; those who prepare the rites must themselves come to grips with the demonic forces from which we pray deliverance over our sisters and brothers who approach full initiation.

PRESENTATION OF CREED/LORD'S PRAYER

Unlike the scrutinies, these rites are somewhat optional in that they may be anticipated and celebrated prior to the Lenten season. The RCIA envisions the Presentation of the Creed during the week after the first scrutiny, and the Presentation of the Lord's Prayer in the week after the third scrutiny. However, many communities have found that this makes for liturgical "overload" and choose to do these rites during the time of the catechumenate. Planners will need to be in dialogue with the catechumenal team on this issue and see to it that whenever the rites are celebrated, they not appear as trivial or of minor importance. These rites, for all of their brevity and simplicity, are among the most venerable and ancient in our liturgical repertoire and express the essence of the initiatory process. In "handing on" the symbols of faith and prayer, a community gives to its members the heart and soul of our Christian way. Although this happens in the many ways that we do our catechumenal formation, we need to ritualize that process with expression and forcefulness in these rites.

FIRST PENANCE FOR CANDIDATES

Those who are baptized candidates for reception into full communion generally seek an experience of the sacrament of penance as part of their Lenten retreat. Provision should be made for them to do so, if they wish, in the context of a communal celebration. Most parishes already have such celebrations as a regular feature of the Lenten season, and relatively little extra effort is required to ensure that the special needs of the candidates are taken into consideration. Planners should make certain that the extra care is given, and that candidates have the best possible experience of this sacrament of healing and peace. The week following the third scrutiny is a "natural" time to celebrate the healing and deliverance that the scrutinies have already set in motion.

RECEPTION INTO FULL COMMUNION

The "White Book" contains a combined rite that allows for reception to occur, together with baptisms, at the Easter vigil. However, many communities have found that this over-crowds the vigil and tends to blur its strong emphasis on baptism. Hence, it is suggested that another time may be more appropriate to celebrate reception. One possibility that has been tried with success is to do the receptions as part of the Holy Thursday celebration. The emphasis on unity among all Christ's followers that is so strong in the Holy Thursday liturgy seems made to order both for ecumenical reasons and as an expression of what reception accomplishes. Confirmation, which leads to the completion of initiation in eucharistic sharing, is similarly at home in the liturgy's themes and moods. If the elect who will be baptized on Saturday are present, as the newly received will also be in attendance at the vigil, then those who have journeyed together at catechumenal sessions do not experience separation or a feeling of being "left out." In fact, planners should make certain that the elect are made to feel included in the Holy Thursday celebration (for example, in the foot washing) just as the newly received will be included at the vigil in some special way.

HOLY SATURDAY PREPARATION RITES

The rites which may be celebrated on Holy Saturday morning require a very delicate hand in order to be done properly. They must be subdued yet substantial, clearly secondary yet not superfluous. What seems important is that they reinforce the atmosphere meant to be generated by the solemn fast of Holy Saturday. The church is waiting, and the elect who feel that wait with intensity and great longing need the support of the community that gathers with them. The mood here is crucial and "less is more," on this occasion especially.

EASTER VIGIL

Those who plan the liturgies of the Lenten season will also want to be involved in the preparation of the vigil. Space precludes treatment of the key issues involved in the planning of this most important of all rites. But readers may wish to consult the author's article on the subject in the Spring 1987 issue of *Church* ("Liturgical Symbols: A Practical Approach," pp. 4-42).

MYSTAGOGY

For the sake of completeness, we mention here the need to plan with the same energy the liturgical rites the RCIA refers to during the Easter season of mystagogy. These are the Sunday Masses of the Easter season, which are celebrated with the neophytes in prominent attendance. As with Lent, so with the Easter season, we are urged to use lectionary Cycle A in which privileged texts proclaim the meaning of initiation. The RCIA is terse in its suggestions for this period, only alluding to "some sort of celebration" to be held near Pentecost Sunday to close the period of postbaptismal catechesis. What a wonderful invitation to creativity!

These remarks have been brief, but I hope suggestive of the scope of the task that liturgical planners face as they seek to implement the rites of the RCIA that surround the Paschal mystery. It is clear that successful planning will need to include explanatory catechesis for assemblies unaccustomed to these new rites. Planning will also need to be comprehensive, attending to details of environment as well as decisions of rite and text. The great ninety days of Lent-Easter will need to be planned as a whole, with valiant effort by all to combat the mystagogical malaise which besets so many communities, who act as if Easter Sunday is end, not beginning.

RITE OF ACCEPTANCE

Implementing the order of Christian initiation of adults presents a new set of ritual challenges to Catholic parishes. Where the catechumenal process is flourishing, it is not unusual for a parish to celebrate the rite of acceptance into the order of catechumens several times a year, as successive groups move from the period of evangelization into the period of the catechumenate. As the U.S. church gains experience with this crucial transitional rite, it accumulates wisdom about what is necessary to celebrate it effectively. The following thoughts are meant to summarize much of that growing practical wisdom.

PREPARATION

Acceptance is not a ritual that can be prepared in the sacristy a few minutes before the celebration begins. It is essential to plan in advance and coordinate plans with the catechumenal team, musicians, readers, greeters, ushers, and others who routinely are involved in the Sunday celebration. Decide whether to enact a joint ritual including both unbaptized and already baptized candidates or to separate the groups and perform two different ceremonies.

The presider will want to meet with the candidates and other members of the catechumenal team to prepare for the rite. Ideally, the preparation includes a catechetical session to prepare the candidates to answer the questions with which the rite begins (What do you ask of God's church? What does faith offer you?). Reflection and sharing brought out in such a session will be of inestimable value to the homilist, who speaks to the larger community about the meaning of this step in the faith journey of the candidates.

The choreography of the rite can be rehearsed with the sponsors and others involved (the director of the catechumenate, cantor, ushers), but ought not to include the candidates themselves. Their role is to experience the rite, without having to worry about forgetting what was taught in rehearsal. To withhold from them beforehand the details of the rite forces them to be more dependent on the lead of their sponsor, which is important at this stage.

GATHERING

How a community gathers for the rite of acceptance is particularly important. The rite allows several options but prefers that the community gather outside the church building. Many parishes find that it is best to have the candidates and sponsors wait outside while the rest of the Sunday assembly gathers inside for a music rehearsal and other preparations; then, just as the candidates begin to feel "left out," the entire assembly emerges from the church singing a simple refrain of welcome, literally surrounding them with the body of Christ. Parishes that have overcome their initial reluctance to try such a dramatic beginning are convinced of its value by the positive effect it has on all concerned. Parishes are rediscovering the importance of processions in this simple way of greeting and welcoming newcomers into the community. It seems worth the effort to make it work well.

OPENING DIALOGUE

The next step is an exchange between candidates and the presider: candidates are introduced by name and asked what they seek from the church. Their answers are best left unrehearsed, spontaneous. If the preparatory catechetical session has helped them to deal with why they are taking this step, they can answer spontaneously from the heart without difficulty. Sponsors and assembly are then questioned about their willingness to support the candidates. An excellent way to involve the whole assembly in the action at each point is to punctuate the answers to the questions with musical acclamations.

Naturally, everyone present should be able to hear what is being said, which may mean using the sound amplification system. The affirmation (called the "first acceptance") made by the candidates, in which they promise to follow Christ and the gospel in the time of preparation (beginning now), can be especially striking.

THE SIGNINGS

The assembly will want to see the signing of the candidates' senses with the cross. For this reason many parishes prefer to move this segment of the ceremony inside now (or later, if the signing occurs after the homily). One of the most ancient catechumenal rituals, the signing has tremendous importance. Its dramatic impact, when carried out fully and expressively, makes it an unforgettable moment in the rite. To enhance visibility, sponsors may spread out in the aisles throughout the assembly area with their candidates. Then, as the presider says the words, sponsors trace the cross on each of the candidate's senses, the forehead, ears, eyes, mouth, shoulders, hands, and feet. Sponsors make the sign with their open palm and actually touch the candidate's body. The effect of such a ritual signing may last a lifetime.

At this part of the rite, some parishes give a small wooden cross to the candidates to be worn around the neck. And to involve the larger assembly more actively, parishes use a judicious selection of short acclamations after each of the signations.

PROCESSION TO HEAR THE WORD

The rite clearly intends the procession to be an evocative symbol of what is occurring in the lives of the catechumens as they "enter the church" for the first time with the rest of the assembly to be nourished on the word of God. The best musicians will select music easy to sing by an assembly moving in procession from outdoors to indoors. The liturgy of the word proceeds as usual once everyone assembles inside.

PRESENTATION OF THE BIBLE

Parishes may choose to give each catechumen a copy of the Bible. The director of the catechumenate may do this after the homily. The presentation is enhanced if the director uses words that respond directly to what each candidate is seeking on his or her journey. If possible, try to use the same words the candidates themselves used earlier in the rite. (The director may need to make notes of such words if there are many candidates.)

PRAYER FOR THE CANDIDATES

Next, the assembly prays a series of intercessions on behalf of the catechumens. A cantor may sing these, adding solemnity and importance to the prayer. At the concluding prayer over the catechumens, presiders may invite the assembly to extend hands in blessing as a way of expressing the truth that all liturgical prayers come from the whole church, not just the presider.

DISMISSAL

The catechumens and catechist go to a place apart where they will pray and reflect further on the word and on what has just taken place. This dismissal is a regular feature of catechetical formation, omitted only by way of exception. Rather than an act of inhospitality, as some parishes fear, it is a gracious invitation to feast on the word more deeply week after week and to experience in the person of the catechist the love and care of the entire assembly. As a symbol of liminality, it is unsurpassed; as an act of ritual catechesis, it says powerfully to the assembly and to the catechumens that the true meaning of initiation is participation at the eucharistic table.

These brief comments only suggest the exciting range of possibilities available to parishes seeking to make this ritual a regular feature of parish life. Creativity and hard work will overcome the symbolic minimalism that still plagues us Catholics in other areas of ritual life. By helping to develop a sense of ritual flow and balance, the order of Christian initiation of adults stirs faith not only in the candidates and catechumens but in the parish at large.

MYSTAGOGY: THE WHO? WHAT? WHEN? WHY? HOW?

Farsighted liturgy committees think beyond the Lenten season to the time of mystagogy. In the early days of the implementation of the Rite of Christian Initiation of Adults, mystagogy was a word known only to a few *cognoscenti*, and practiced by even fewer. It seemed mostly to be the concern of beleaguered catechists already burned-out by the rigors of Lent and the exhilaration of the Easter vigil. These are more mature times, however, and today parishes without new members being initiated at the vigil are in the minority. In most parishes the days between Easter and Pentecost are no longer just the "Easter season." Rather, they are the time of postbaptismal catechesis or mystagogy, when the entire community is called to participate in the final stage of adult initiation. This is not just another challenge to the creativity and stamina of the parish catechists. While the period of mystagogy is an important time of catechesis, indeed, it is primarily ritual in form, and the principal catechist is the liturgical assembly itself. This understanding is something of a shift.

Ten years ago, those working to implement the rites of adult initiation thought of mystagogy as a period of special instruction on sacraments to be given to neophytes at their regular weekly meetings. They also introduced the neophytes to parish groups and signed them up for particular parish ministries. A more careful reading of the text of the rite – and more thoughtful reflection on the ancient roots of mystagogical experience – have helped to refocus this final stage of initiation. Mystagogy is now thought of as primarily a ritual experience. The normative form of mystagogical catechesis is given shape within the Sunday Eucharist by the homilist and the assembly during the great fifty days of Easter. Of course, other pastoral activities are appropriate during this time. In the yearlong period of postbaptismal formation mandated by the American bishops, the initiation team will still need to be creative in its efforts to help neophytes find a fruitful place to serve within the parish community. But the mystagogy is most properly experienced at the Sunday gathering of the community for Eucharist.

MEETING THE RISEN CHRIST

This liturgical vision takes seriously the formative power of the liturgical seasons. Vatican II (CSL, #102) went so far as to say that the annual liturgical cycle is one of the ways that the mystery of Christ is made present and unfolds within the community of believers. We are gradually coming to understand that at least as much time and energy must be spent on the period of mystagogy as on Lent. The challenge is for a worshiping community (as well as its neophytes) to be surrounded by powerful symbols and involved in rituals during mystagogy and thus come to "know" experientially the meaning of the life of the Risen One that is being celebrated.

Liturgy planners have as their responsibility the task of helping believers experience and understand during this time the Lord's Resurrection. Mystagogy reminds us that it is in the sacraments – especially the sacraments of initiation – that a Christian most fully encounters the Risen Christ in an immediate and deeply personal fashion. The fifty days of Easter are the church's prolonged meditation on how we have come to share in the life of Christ as a result of our immersion into the waters of rebirth, our anointing with the Spirit, and our feasting at the eucharistic table. The period of mystagogy is a time of catechesis for the entire community, not only the neophytes, during which the central fact of Christian experience is meditated upon and celebrated.

START WITH THE TEXTS

The place for liturgy planners to begin, as with every liturgical season, is with the "texts" provided us by the church. This means the lectionary in a preeminent way, of course, and the prayers of the sacramentary. Those inclined to explore more deeply the meaning of the season will want to look at the wealth of material contained in the liturgy of the hours as well. Reading these sources, praying and reflecting on them, and sharing one another's understanding will surely help any group of liturgy planners come to a deeper appreciation of the major concerns of the season as they are unfolded over the course of seven weeks.

The homilist's role is specific and crucial during the period of mystagogy. (The classic examples of mystagogical catechesis are episcopal homilies delivered during Easter week.) For this reason, it seems particularly important that the parish's liturgy planners be in dialogue with the homilist(s) who will have such a key responsibility. The scriptural texts in the lectionary cycle A have been selected specifically for use with communities with newly initiated members. It is hard to imagine not exercising the recommendation of the rite that cycle A be used whenever a community enjoys the presence of neophytes.

NEOPHYTES AS SYMBOLS

Many communities have found great benefit in asking the neophytes themselves to give witness to their new experience of the Lord's presence in their lives. This could be done as part of a dialogue with the homilist or perhaps after Communion. However it is arranged, the newly initiated should speak from deeply personal experience about how encountering Christ in the sacraments has "made a difference" for them.

The neophytes, recognizing how their own experience becomes a mirror for the rest of the community's reflection, will come to understand that they are providing a service by allowing themselves to be held up as living symbols of the transforming power of Christ's Paschal mystery. They will gladly witness to their faith and share their joy, because they will see how enriching such moments can be for the entire community.

The rite of adult initiation reminds us that the neophytes themselves are primary symbols during mystagogia. This is why the rite suggests that they may sit in a special place in the assembly with their godparents and receive special mention during the general intercessions. Some communities have even asked them to wear their white baptismal garments each Sunday of Easter, as did their ancient predecessors daily throughout Easter week.

Other communities ask the neophytes and their families to present the gifts each week until Pentecost – a gesture of striking significance for those who over many months (and even years) have grown accustomed to seeing those to be initiated dismissed from the assembly after the homily. Watching the newly initiated remain, bring up the gifts of bread and wine, and then approach the eucharistic table with the rest of the faithful is a forceful experience of ritual catechesis for the entire community.

Thanks to the rite of adult initiation, we see more clearly that the fifty days of Easter are about being incorporated into the life of the Risen Christ, especially through the sacraments of initiation. Eucharist, as the "repeatable sacrament of initiation" (Augustine), is the heart of all mystagogy.

THE GREAT CONFIRMATION DEBATE

Joe and Mary are devoted Catholics, trying their best to raise their four children in accord with the teachings of the church. They live in a large metropolitan area where the borders of three dioceses intersect. Because of a series of moves to larger and better homes over the last several years Joe and Mary have resided within all three of the neighboring dioceses.

Five years ago they lived in a diocese where policy called for confirmation during eighth grade. Their son Jimmy pre-

pared for the sacrament as part of his regular religious instruction class in the parochial school. The school routinely
prepared all eighth graders to celebrate confirmation, much
as it does with the sacraments of first penance and first
Eucharist for those in second grade.

The next year, however, Joe and Mary moved and were
quite surprised to find out that their new parish celebrated
confirmation at the time of first Eucharist. There, they were
required to prepare their daughter Susan at home for the
sacraments of penance, confirmation, and Eucharist. Sacramental preparation classes were held for parents only. This
parish stressed that the family is the proper setting in which
to prepare children to complete their sacramental initiation.

Again this year, in a new parish and a new diocese, Joe
and Mary have discovered that diocesan policy decrees confirmation to be a sacrament of maturity restricted to young
adults in senior high school. Preparation requires two years'
involvement in a total youth ministry program complete with
service projects, spiritual formation at retreats, and so forth.
Because of the nature of adolescence as a time of rebellion
against parents, preparation for the sacrament involves more
emphasis on peer interaction than parental involvement.

PASTORAL CHAOS

While this scenario is fictitious, the sad truth is that it could
easily be true. It seems that the one clear and indisputable
characteristic of the church's current experience of confirmation is that we are immersed in widespread pastoral chaos.
Contradictory theologies are taught as "gospel"; diverse
catechetical approaches are embraced with uncritical enthusiasm; diocesan policies and episcopal leadership run the
gamut from rigid demands for conformity to *laissez-faire*
experimentation; pastoral practice on the parish level resembles an Oriental bazaar more than a coherent vision of sacramental initiation into the Catholic tradition.

AN IMMODEST PROPOSAL

To offer a solution amid such chaos might seem to be singularly immodest. Nonetheless, I am convinced that the way out of this chaos is available to us if we are guided by good historical research, long-standing liturgical tradition, critical theological reflection, clear direction from Roman canonical legislation, and tested pastoral wisdom. Space restraints prevent me from presenting all of the evidence that could be mustered to support my case. But I do offer here a series of assertions that captures the essence of the argument, which, I believe, must be made more in detail elsewhere.

• *Our sacramental rituals have a history that must not be ignored.* Christian meanings encoded in ritual symbols are linked to the specific story of Jesus and reflect a particular history. The traditional belief that sacraments are instituted by Christ was a way of saying what still holds true: we cannot tamper with the meanings connected to our sacramental history. We are not free to make of confirmation whatever we will, simply because we feel the sacrament will be more meaningful if it is presented with a different theological rationale.

• *The history of the sacrament of confirmation demonstrates irrefutably that it is a sacrament of initiation not of maturity.* The genesis of this ritual of anointing and laying on of hands is inextricably linked to the water bath which precedes it and to the Eucharist which follows. At its inception and throughout its history, confirmation has been and remains a part of Christian initiation. It is indeed a "rite of passage," but it is a passage from baptism into Eucharist, not from childhood into some arbitrarily constructed developmental stage of "maturity."

• *Restoring the integrity of the sequence (baptism-confirmation-Eucharist) of the sacraments of initiation is critically important on historical, liturgical, theological, and pastoral grounds.* The reasons why we must restore the original sequence are not trivial. They embody many of our core values about the nature of church and sacrament and our understanding of how the sacramental economy reflects the Trinitarian economy of salvation.

What is at stake are the initiatory and the Paschal "contexts," both of which are essential to the preservation of a sound theology of the sacrament. When the proper sequence is lost, the Trinitarian balance is upset, a situation that has very practical implications: catechists and theologians must scramble to "explain" just exactly where and how and when one is joined to Christ and endowed with the Spirit. The result is pastoral chaos.

• *Arguments for confirmation as a sacrament of maturity are fundamentally flawed in that they are based on a defective notion of what constitutes sacramental "readiness."* Developmental readiness is a crucial factor to keep in mind in all catechetical efforts, including preparation for any of the seven sacraments. However, readiness for the sacraments of initiation involves more than catechetical considerations. Theological and ecclesiological considerations are of primary importance, as is shown so clearly by the church's ancient practice of initiating even infants.

Many arguments for the delay of confirmation until the end of grade school or high school reinforce coercive elements of religious formation and make it "sacramental bait" to keep youngsters involved in programs they would not otherwise choose freely. This is an abuse of the sacraments and reveals a pastoral approach that is morally bankrupt. It is the destruction of all that our sacraments are about.

• *Legislation implementing Vatican II's reform of the sacraments of initiation consistently points the way out of the present pastoral chaos.* There is an overwhelming body of conciliar, liturgical, and canonical legislation, which makes clear that the preferred Roman practice is confirmation restored as a sacrament of initiation. The documentation is immense, making it incredible that it is so little known or so often ignored. The Roman reform envisions confirmation as a sacrament of initiation conferred between baptism and first Eucharist, presumably at the time of first Eucharist.

As a concession to those seeking pastoral flexibility, Rome gave permission for episcopal conferences to choose another age for confirmation – in order to accommodate exceptional circumstances. But that permission to choose a single alternative age has been distorted by our own episcopal conference. The conference has interpreted the law as allowing each bishop to set a different diocesan policy.

PASTORAL CARE

There are, of course, no villains in this tale of shifting confirmation practices that have led to widespread pastoral chaos. Rather, one can identify understandable historical factors that separated confirmation from baptism in the first place. More recently, in this century, when the liturgical reform of Pius X lowered the age for first Eucharist, confirmation at a later age was left "hanging" in some places. We are all familiar with the heroic attempts of catechists and others to deal with such unintended displacement.

But what has happened is no longer a question of making a virtue out of necessity. Vatican II reform has called the entire church – bishops, theologians, catechists, parents, and pastors – to a better, more authentic, and ultimately more life-giving practice with regard to the sacrament of confirmation. Proper pastoral care requires that we respect the broad consistency of the reform-illustrated in the revised rituals of infant baptism, confirmation, and especially the Christian initiation of adults, all of which envision confirmation as a sacrament of initiation. True pastoral care will embrace that vision of reform and work toward a restoration of confirmation to its proper place within initiation. Failure to do so for whatever reason – episcopal timidity, theological naiveté, catechetical obstinacy, liturgical insensitivity, or pastoral lethargy – will result in poor pastoral care of God's people.

VI.

THE EUCHARISTIC LITURGY

GATHERING FOR WORSHIP

Despite how little attention we pay to it, the manner in which we gather for worship is extremely important. Architects, cultural anthropologists, and sociologists are keenly aware of the significance of how people gather together for important occasions. Often, however, those who worship in the parish have little or no such awareness. This is remarkable because theologically, the notion of gathering has a central place in our traditional understanding of who we are as a community of faith. The ancient Hebrew word *qahal* (the Greek equivalent is *ekklesia*) finds its modern counterpart in the term assembly, or church, designating the gathering of God's people. Those terms are rich in both history and meaning, carrying within them the story of how God called a chosen people, first to the Mosaic covenant and then also to the new covenant forged in the blood of Jesus.

When we come together to worship *we are* the gathering, the community of God's chosen ones. We assemble precisely because we wish to respond in faith to the grace of God that we have received. How we gather, then, is an expression of who we are. For this reason, parish liturgy committees will find it helpful to reflect on how their community currently gathers for worship, and how they might gather in ways that better reflect their deepest identity as Christians.

IT STARTS SOONER THAN YOU THINK

In a very real sense, one's entire week serves as the prelude and influences mightily how we gather for worship. We come to Mass every Sunday carrying with us (like a sack of rocks or, perhaps, a bright bouquet of flowers) the joys and sorrows, the triumphs and failures of the week just past. Imagine the difference in the ways that two people might gather for worship on a Sunday morning: one, who has spent a few quiet moments every day reading and praying over the Sunday readings and the other, whose week has been steeped in pornographic reading and television violence. Might not a parish liturgy committee be a place where ideas could surface regarding how the community can help its members gather with minds and hearts *ready* to listen to God's word and respond with offerings of praise and thanksgiving? Such a discussion might well result in a decision to start Scripture sharing groups during the week to explain and discuss the coming Sunday's readings.

More immediately, the way a community gathers is very much influenced by the patterns of leave-taking and making transitions that characterize how individuals and families leave home and come to church. Parents have told me that they very deliberately use the time in the car between home and church to discuss with their children the readings they are about to hear or some other topic designed to help them better enter into the Sunday celebration. Other parents have complained about how hard it is to be in the right frame of mind for church when their departure from home has been like a pitched battle. I suspect that commuter parishes, where virtually everyone arrives by car, have a much different pattern of gathering than parishes where everyone arrives on foot. In the latter, it makes a difference whether people have strolled through lovely surrounding neighborhoods or through streets infested with drugs and crime. Parish liturgy committees need to be aware of such patterns in their community and how these can be addressed to help worshipers gather in the best possible way.

WHAT HAPPENS OUTSIDE MATTERS

When liturgy committees discuss the environment for worship, they usually focus on the interior of the church building. But architects and city planners know better, and we are well advised to follow their wisdom in considering the physical environment that greets people first when they arrive at the church property. For example, we cannot afford to ignore traffic flow. If people must make a hazardous left turn in the face of oncoming traffic just to enter the parking lot, that experience will adversely influence their frame of mind for more than a few seconds. If the parking lot is congested, causing tempers regularly to flare over too few spaces or narrow lanes, that experience will influence those who gather. If people must walk through mud when it rains or over sidewalks habitually icy or snow covered rather than carefully scraped and dry, such experiences will influence them as worship begins. If the parish property is unkempt, worshipers will feel different from parishioners whose parish reflects pride in its appearance. If a family has spent several hours on Saturday morning planting beautiful flowers in front of the parish entrance, not only they, but hundreds of others as well, will gather in a brighter mood. Ancient Roman basilicas often had lush gardens with flowing fountains that worshipers passed through on their way inside. This was to evoke an image of the Garden of Eden and provide a space of quiet and beauty that would prepare the worshipers properly for the ensuing celebration. Liturgy committees that are sensitive to these matters will quickly make contact with the "grounds committee" (or its equivalent) to address such issues.

GREETING AND WELCOMING

As important as the physical considerations are, they pale before the significance of the human encounter. Hospitality is a virtue so deeply a part of the Christian experience that one is at a loss to understand why it is still so little in evidence when Catholics gather for worship. Nothing is more basic to hospitality than the act of greeting and welcoming, yet in countless Catholic churches there is simply no effort devoted to this most fundamental human need. If we gather without giving attention to the strangers in our midst (let alone those who are family, that is, the most familiar), then we proclaim a message contrary to the Gospel.

If how we gather says something about who we are (and it does!), then we have no choice but to take care in greeting and welcoming all who come to worship.

The liturgy committee will want to examine how well the details of hospitality are being attended to, taking whatever steps are needed to ensure that each person who gathers is recognized as the Christ in our midst. The possibilities this opens up are vast. Some communities have instituted the ministry of "greeter" to address this need rather than add to the job description of the ushers. Many parishes, realizing the importance of hospitality, have made their buildings more accessible to the disabled, often at a cost of thousands of dollars. The committee will want to look carefully at how greeting takes place.

- Are the greeters visible and clearly identifiable?
- Where should they stand in relation to the doors?
- Are they trained to be alert and help strangers to feel comfortable?
- Should they be giving out bulletins or music books?

The primary consideration is to extend a welcome to every person as we would welcome Christ.

ATMOSPHERE IN THE WORSHIP SPACE

The atmosphere encountered upon entering a place of worship sends a strong message. Current customs vary widely in this regard. In some churches the hushed quiet makes even a whispered greeting to a neighbor likely to seem out of place. Other communities gather with a buzz of conversation and mutual greeting that makes for a festive, exuberant atmosphere. Such differences usually reflect strongly held attitudes and understandings sometimes charged with more emotion than thoughtfulness. Ideological stances may quickly surface if there is an attempt to alter the status quo, but that does not mean the liturgy committee should avoid discussing the issue. For some people, an atmosphere of quiet in the presence of the Blessed Sacrament is essential, providing those who gather time for prayerful recollection. Others prefer a gathering time in which the community connects with one another in warm (and inevitably noisy) ways. Each parish must decide for itself what atmosphere it wishes to maintain as people gather. The decision ought to be made not on the basis of private piety, but of what best serves the community worship.

HELPING THE ASSEMBLY TO PREPARE

I think that shortly before the formal liturgical ritual begins, the community usually needs some help in preparing those present for their role in the celebration. Most often, this will be provided by a songleader, but it might also be the presider or someone else with appropriate skills. Several things need to happen at this point:

- People should be invited to stop what they have been doing (whether quietly praying or chatting with friends) in order to focus their attention on the leader.
- Words of welcome should be extended to those present. In some communities this might simply be a "good

morning." In other places, extended welcomes with introduction of visitors, etc., might be appropriate.

- The assembly should have a musical warm-up. This might involve teaching new music or reviewing (for visitors) some of the basics. This step is important and should not be neglected. Just as the members of a choir would never be asked to perform without warming up their voices, so the members of a liturgical assembly should never be asked to sing without warming up their voices. This has the added benefit of helping to establish the cohesiveness of the assembly, which will momentarily be asked to serve as a sign of the unity of the Body of Christ.

- The leader should provide any other information or preparation the assembly might need (for example, explanations about some special ritual) in order to participate fully.

- By way of conclusion, the leader will invite the assembly to prepare themselves for worship, perhaps by calling for reflective quiet, or by inviting them to listen to a prelude by the choir, or by asking them to stand and join in the gathering song.

These remarks about gathering all have to do with what occurs *before* the start of what is known as the gathering rites. However, the success of the gathering rites, indeed, of the entire liturgical celebration, is related to how well a community gathers in the larger sense. Those responsible for the liturgical life of a parish would be well advised to think broadly along these lines as they ponder how best to help each assembly worship in spirit and in truth.

LITURGY OF THE WORD

Liturgy committees that take a serious look at their parish's experience of Sunday worship are often tempted to the sin of despair. Honest evaluation all too frequently reveals a fairly grim situation, and "we don't know where to begin" is but a short step from "it's hopeless." The answer, of course, is that begin we must, somewhere. I am often asked where I think is the most important place to begin improving a community's Sunday liturgical celebration. My answer is nearly always: the Liturgy of the Word.

No other element in the liturgical mix is as readily susceptible to improvement, and there are few rivals in terms of immediate payoffs for even minor changes. Other aspects of the liturgy, such as music, are equally crucial and yield significant gains when improvements occur. But they are generally more complex and difficult to tackle. Begin with working on the Liturgy of the Word, I urge, and you'll experience dramatic results.

The following is a quick survey and summary of the major features that a committee would wish to consider in developing a plan for improving the Liturgy of the Word. For parishes that are already down the road a piece in liturgical revival, it may serve as a convenient examination of conscience to review how things are going.

RECRUITMENT OF READERS

It is important that the ministry of reader be exercised by a mix of persons representative of the parish at large. In recruiting to achieve that balance, personal invitations are best, always with a qualifier about the need to see if one's public reading skills are sufficient to the task. Screening of prospective readers is an essential, since not everyone has the specific talents required for public proclamation of the Scriptures. Without imposing rigorous standards, a parish can reasonably insist on some minimal level of skill in order to qualify for this ministry.

TRAINING OF READERS

While initial training is an obvious necessity and should be done with some fair amount of time and effort, the need for training does not end there. Regular rehearsal before each assignment is the expected norm, and parishes that have insisted on this as a policy can witness to the dramatic improvements that result. If an experienced person like the president of the United States still rehearses his delivery before major speeches, it seems more than justifiable to make rehearsal and critique a weekly feature of parish life for those who proclaim the Sunday readings. In addition, special training events should be scheduled during the course of the year, both for skill building and spiritual formation for ministry. Training, in other words, must become a normal and significant component of the ministry of readers.

CHOREOGRAPHY OF THE RITE

Like any ritual performance, the Liturgy of the Word involves choreographed movement and gesture that need to be thoughtfully designed and executed. Readers should know how to take their part in the entrance procession, as well as how to carry and handle the book with reverence. Seating of readers with the assembly, rather than in the sanctuary, seems to express better the origin of this ministry in the community. But this requires attention to the way movement happens to and from the ambo: neither rushed nor artificially slow, in a relaxed manner that does not call undue attention to the movement. The custom of readers remaining at the ambo for a period of silence after the proclamation also serves as a model for the assembly that this is a time for quiet reflection, not distracting movement. We would hope that by now parishes would have complied with the directives in the lectionary to have two separate readers for the first and second readings, as a way of respecting the important principle of diversification of ministries.

SOUND AND SILENCE

It seems an incredibly obvious necessity, but still one encounters parishes where the amplification system is inadequate to the task of public proclamation. Suffice it to say, any serious concern with the quality of the Liturgy of the Word must ensure that the sound is crisp and clear to all in the assembly. Those who use the system must also know how to do so properly, of course. In these days when so few things seem to merit the label "mortal sin," we ought to charge with that offense all who permit the word to be read but neither heard nor understood! Just as important as adequate sound is adequate silence. Readers ought to be as staunch as the conductor of the local orchestra in their refusal to begin until silence reigns. The concert music is too important to begin with any noisy competition from latecomers or restless fidgeting. So is our sacred Scripture. Equally crucial is the hushed calm that should prevail immediately after the proclamation. If we truly believe we've said something of value, we need to provide that quiet space for contemplation and assimilation of the word.

SING THE SONGS

Imagine the opening of a ball game where the crowd stands to recite "The Star Spangled Banner." Utterly absurd and ludicrous! We ought to feel the same level of discomfort with the suggestion that we recite the responsorial psalm or the gospel verse. Sing the songs; it's as simple as that.

BOOKS

The major book to be carried in procession and receive special reverence is the book of the Gospels, now finally published as a separate volume in handsome binding. Failing that, a full lectionary is an adequate second choice. Those who continue to proclaim the sacred Scriptures from shoddy paperbacks are probably the same sinners who perpetrate poor sound systems, and theirs is a sin of equal magnitude. The great missalette debate continues to rage, despite an increasingly clear appreciation of the issues involved. Missalettes are wonderful, even necessary helps for the hearing-impaired. Given to the parish at large as a take-home tool, they encourage preparation and review of the Sunday readings. But as something to be followed during the proclamation, they are as appropriate as a suitor handing his beloved the text of the marriage proposal he is about to make. Our liturgical and faith traditions insist that the Liturgy of the Word is a speech event, a proclamatory moment, an interpersonal call, and not a careful simultaneous reading of an ancient document, however important the text.

HOMILIES

Surveys have pretty definitely documented the concern of most Catholics over the quality of the preached word that they hear week after week. It would be foolhardy to ignore this major issue in any attempt to improve a parish's experience of the Liturgy of the Word. But by now it has also become clear that more priest-bashing won't help the situation. Most priests know they could improve and desperately want to. Few, however, have found good ways to do so, despite some tested evidence of what actually works. First, let the parish give him more time in his weekly schedule to pray, to exegete the text, and to work on preparation. Convince him that the parish would rather have him do those things than fix boilers or be a business manager. Convince him by changing the system that often leaves him holding the bag on those other things. Convince him by tangible, dramatic proof in the form of concrete help. That help can take the form of lifting administrative burdens as well as offers to join in such efforts as Scripture-sharing groups and faith-sharing sessions where staff or parishioners discuss the lectionary readings and try to make connections with their real lives. Help him with constructive feedback about what works and what doesn't, and support him with enough affirmation and understanding to make him willing to risk trying out some new approaches.

COMMITMENT OF PARISH RESOURCES

If we are to make the Liturgy of the Word a real priority, we need to reflect that commitment through our allocations of resources. That generally means time, money, talent, people, schedules, spaces, and so forth. Adult education in the parish needs to develop strategies to help folks know and live the Scriptures more deeply. This will mean speakers and courses and materials and study groups and faith sharing. We need to become a people of the word. What was alluded to earlier regarding training obviously implies a significant allocation of resources. The fact is, we will invest in what really matters to us. And regardless of any protestations to the contrary, it will be clear whether or not the proclamation of the word is for us a matter of great value.

LITURGY OF THE WORD FOR CHILDREN

In recent years growing numbers of parishes around the country have begun to add a Liturgy of the Word for children to their Sunday eucharistic celebrations. These are special gatherings of young children, apart from the main assembly, where the young are able to hear the Scriptures proclaimed and explained in language accommodated to their own developmental level. Because this phenomenon has spread so rapidly and with very little pastoral direction, it seems timely to offer here some basic guidance for communities wishing to implement this practice.

CONSULTING THE DIRECTORY

The Directory for Masses with Children is the Roman document that authorizes and encourages the practice of special celebrations of the word for children where adaptation to their special needs is possible. That wonderfully forward-looking document should be read carefully and reflectively by those who are entrusted with responsibility for developing a children's liturgy. I will not repeat here all of the details which the directory contains, but urge you thoroughly to assimilate and implement its vision. Instead, I will describe what such a gathering might look like and offer suggestions for ensuring high standards of liturgical celebration.

TAKING CHILDREN'S WORSHIP SERIOUSLY

It is essential that the community, at every level, consider such celebrations to be every bit as important as the proclamation of the word which occurs in the main assembly. The temptation exists to consider the children's experience not as important as the adult celebration. Nothing could be further from the truth! This means that the community's allocation of resources must reflect the importance such celebrations deserve.

The space that is used, for example, should be given careful consideration by those entrusted with shaping the liturgical environment of the celebration. Because the space will usually be something originally intended for another purpose, its adaptation to liturgical use will require creativity and determined effort. If a classroom is chosen, it should be made to appear distinctive – not just as another classroom.

Liturgical colors, worthy furnishings (e.g., an ambo), and decorative arts can signal to the children that this is now a place of worship. Similarly, the lectionary from which the word is proclaimed must be a volume of substance and dignity as befits the word of God.

A LECTIONARY FOR CHILDREN

The U.S. bishops have recently authorized publication of a children's lectionary which contains a complete cycle of readings for the entire three-year lectionary cycle. It is virtually certain that even with the published editions of the approved *Lectionary for Children,* some local communities will still be making adaptations to suit specific needs. One can only hope that such efforts are done with the care and caution that befits any effort to render the word of God faithfully in a language other than the original. Past experience has already shown the disastrous results when good-willed but uninformed volunteers try to tamper with the Scripture to "make it clearer" for the children, often betraying the very meaning of the original passage. Ignorance of the complexities involved in translation and of the theological issues that underlie the passages we read on Sunday morning is no excuse for the blunders that are so frequently made.

GATHERING AND RE-GATHERING

Most communities have children gather with the main assembly for the opening rites of the Mass. This seems a wise move since it emphasizes the basic unity of the Sunday assembly. After the opening prayer of the day, the presider calls forward the children and those adults who will be their ministers of the word. A very brief admonition, to the children to be attentive and to the adult ministers to perform their ministry with care, seems a good way to remind everyone of what is at stake. This little dialogue should take less than a minute and conclude with words of dismissal, much as is done later, after the homily, with the catechumens. The dismissal should take the form of a solemn liturgical procession, perhaps led by cross or candle bearers.

Once you have gathered the children in the place where they will hear the word proclaimed, you will usually need to refocus their attention. This can be done quickly and easily by having the leader call for silence, followed by a prayer or, perhaps, by singing a song. The regathering should be brief, allowing for a quick transition into the proclamation of the first reading. Pastoral considerations will determine how many readings are actually proclaimed. As a bare minimum, read at least the gospel. Except with the very youngest children, it seems appropriate to select another text as well. The lector – just as the lectors in the main assembly – should be well prepared beforehand. It is ideal if the children themselves are capable of proclaiming the word at this point. But if that cannot be done effectively, a qualified and prepared adult should do so.

TEACH CHILDREN TO SING THE PSALMS

After the first reading, sing a psalm. This is not a trivial matter. We need to start forming early on an awareness that sung psalmody is at the heart of our Catholic way of prayer. If suitable cantors cannot be prepared to proclaim the verses, the verses might be read while everyone sings the refrain. Singing is so important to children's spiritual formation that it is impossible to emphasize enough how essential it is to work toward a strong singing of the psalms. Many communities use special children's music for this psalmody. I am of the opinion that it is better to pick music already familiar from its use in the main assembly. The ultimate aim of special liturgies for children is to enhance their later incorporation into the adult assembly. Thus, it makes good sense to use music that will allow them to feel at home when they return to the main assembly. Also, seasonal refrains used repeatedly at Mass are good to teach to children so that they become accustomed to them and develop a love for them. Certainly, every community can have a hearty version of the alleluia that children can sing as a gospel acclamation.

PREACHING FOR CHILDREN

After the proclamation of the gospel, the presiding minister is to give a homily. It is at this point that many communities make a serious mistake. All too often the leader reverts to a catechetical rather than a liturgical mode, giving the children a "lesson" much as might happen in a religious education class, rather than a true homily. It cannot be insisted strongly enough that the children's celebration is liturgy, hence, the appropriate discourse is homiletic, not catechetical. This is a particularly challenging task for the leaders, most of whom have usually been trained as catechists. It is also a challenge to those persons preparing the leaders, for they must instill in the leaders not only presiding skills, but also effective skills in preaching to young children. Commercially published materials for children's liturgies of the word are woefully lacking on this account. For the most part, they offer suggestions that are clearly out of the catechetical mode, rather than the liturgical.

"Fulfilled in Your Hearing," the little booklet on the homily in the Sunday assembly published by the National Conference of Catholic Bishops, is an excellent resource to put into the hands of those adults who will give homilies to children. Although it is aimed at preachers in the adult assembly, its principles are basic and its sound advice can be followed by presiders at children's celebrations as well. Even when interactive techniques such as dialogues and prepared activities are used to accommodate the shorter attention span of young children, the preacher must not lose the integrity of the homily as a time to unfold the meaning of the Scriptures and apply them to daily life.

After the homily, it is important to follow the structure of the Liturgy of the Word from the main assembly, allowing, of course, for accommodations made to the children's developmental level. That means inviting a profession of faith in some form, followed by intercessory prayer. It is not advisable to have the children recite the entire Nicene Creed, given its complex language and thought structure. An alternative might be the Apostles' Creed or even a simple "I do" in response to the questions used at the renewal of baptismal promises. Or, perhaps just a single phrase of the creed might be explained and then repeated by the children, so that over a period of time they would become familiar with the entire text. The intercessory prayer that follows can invite the children's involvement by spontaneous petitions. It is also an ideal time to school them in the four categories of concern that mark the structure of the general intercessions, for example, "Children, what would you like to ask God for as we remember the needs of our church . . . of our leaders. . . ."

CELEBRATING EUCHARIST

Following the conclusion of the word celebration, the children return in liturgical procession to the main assembly in time for the liturgy of the Eucharist. Some communities, instead of returning all of the children at this time, send back only those youngsters who have already received their first Eucharist. In such a case, those who are in the children's catechumenate and those baptized in infancy who have not yet received their first Eucharist remain behind for appropriate catechesis until the conclusion of Mass.

We are still in the very earliest stages of implementing the suggestions of the *Directory for Masses with Children* regarding special celebrations of the Liturgy of the Word for children. However, there is already great enthusiasm and excitement around the country for the promise this practice holds. I hope my remarks highlight the importance of the

practice and its proper implementation. The oft quoted principle of the U.S. bishops holds true for children as well as
for adults: "Good celebrations foster and nourish faith. Poor
celebrations weaken and destroy it" (*Music in Catholic Worship,* 6).

RITE OF BLESSING AND SPRINKLING

Many parish liturgy committees have found it helpful to
organize their work by focusing occasionally on very specific
segments of a given liturgical ritual. We offer here some ideas
which can assist in such an effort of evaluation and reflection
on the Sunday rite of blessing and sprinkling holy water. It
goes without saying, of course, that this specific attention to
one element in the Sunday eucharistic celebration will eventually have to be integrated into a broader set of concerns
affecting the Sunday liturgy as a whole.

IMPORTANCE OF INTRODUCTIONS

We all know from personal experience how important first
impressions can be. The whole complex of ritual actions that
make up the "introductory rites" of the Sunday celebration
have as their purpose "is to help the faithful who have come
together in one place to make themselves into a worshiping
community and to engender the dispositions they should have
when listening to God's word and celebrating the Eucharist"
(GIRM, #24). These diverse elements, if choreographed well,
can effectively gather the assembly into an attitude of prayerful, attentive unity, ready to listen with heart and mind to
the proclamation of the word. Or, they can easily set a mood
of confusion, boredom, distraction, or worse.

The introductory rites are clearly meant to be secondary
when compared to the primary hinges of word and sacrament.
But within this context, considerable latitude is still possible,

from the customary rhythm of ordinary time – usually brisk
and relatively brief – to the more elaborate, fuller expression
which may be suitable on more solemn occasions. In penitential times, it may be appropriate to scale back the introductory rites to a more stark and sober setting. In deciding
whether and how to do the rite of blessing and sprinkling,
one should give careful consideration to its place within the
series of elements that comprise the introductory rites, which,
in turn, should be assessed for their impact on the overall
celebration.

INVITATION TO PRAYER

The sacramentary directs the presider to invite the assembly
into prayer with words of his own choosing. As in all of the
other places where words may be freely composed, this is not
an opportunity for spontaneous remarks. Thoughtful preparation beforehand will guide the presider as to what should
be spoken and how. This is the place where the assembly is
helped to enter into the proper context for the rite. The
presider establishes a preliminary hermeneutic of the ritual
by brief words which evoke theme, mood, frame of mind,
or attitude of heart. Like any good symbol, this ritual action
is inexhaustibly rich and can hold many meanings. In Lent,
the presider may wish to focus on its cleansing and purificatory elements; in Easter season, on its potential for renewal
of baptismal commitment; on other occasions, its linkages
with a particular feast or set of readings. If the presider is not
highly skilled in evoking such nuances, the parish liturgy
committee may be able to identify someone who can prepare
remarks that he can use as text or model for his own composition. As always, less is more, especially in our already
excessively verbal introductory rites. A few well-turned
phrases, filled with words that are poetic and evocative, seem
to be the ideal here. If, in fact, the invitation to prayer has
"worked," the assembly will be still and silent and actually

praying, not waiting to "get on with it." After ample time for quiet prayer, the presider pronounces the assembly's words of blessing over the water.

BLESSING OF THE WATER

Liturgical history has demonstrated the importance of the prayers of blessing over water in our tradition. The sacramentary offers three versions, one for use during Easter season and two for other times. All of them resonate with the imagery and themes of the great blessing from the Easter vigil. The proclamation of this blessing is an important moment in the ritual and should be experienced as such. Musically gifted presiders may sing the prayer; those not so talented may read it solemnly, with appropriate underscoring by the musician; some assemblies may find it works better to punctuate the prayer with sung acclamations. Given the importance of the text, caution should be exercised in any adaptations. Those communities that decide to adapt the language of the blessing prayer should be careful to respect the importance of the elements invoking the Holy Spirit and recalling the mediation of Jesus, which are integral to the structure of blessing in our tradition.

SPRINKLING THE WATER

Once the word of blessing has transformed the water into sacred symbol, its dispersion throughout the assembly becomes a crucial ritual action. A community's sensitivity to the importance of full, robust symbol is inevitably put to the test at this point. Horror stories abound of presiders who never leave the sanctuary and offer only a limp-wristed shake of the aspergellum in the direction of the assembly. What is needed here is for the assembly to experience flowing water – the life-giving kind described by Jesus in his encounter with the Samaritan woman at the well. Few aspergella, no matter how ornate, are up to the task. Most frequently, assemblies that wish to disperse the water far and wide have found that a simple tree branch works best. Some more innovative communities have sought a fuller expression by blessing several bowls of water. These are then held by ministers as the community comes forward in procession (as during Communion), or they are passed down the rows, like collection baskets. Musical accompaniment to this ritual action seems essential in order to avoid any sense of "dead space." Song or acclamation may be chosen that supports the presider's initial remarks, or the assembly may simply do a verse or two of the song used for the entrance procession. What seems essential in all of this is that the entire assembly be engaged in an action that allows each person to experience the gift of life-giving water, poured out in our midst as a saving sign of God's continuing presence.

ABSOLUTION/CONCLUDING PRAYER

The ritual concludes with a final prayer by the presider. The text provided in the sacramentary makes clear the strongly purificatory character of these words of absolution. What seems most appropriate is that they be spoken clearly and crisply, with a sense of finality that brings closure to the entire ritual. To enhance this text by singing does not seem advisable, since it should not compete with the rite's major emphasis on blessing and sprinkling. It is, in a sense, declaratory commentary on what has transpired rather than a climactic moment of forgiveness.

We have suggested in these remarks the importance of thoughtful preparation of the rite of blessing and sprinkling of holy water. Careful consideration must be given to this potentially powerful ritual action if it is to "fit" well in the Sunday celebration. We have suggested some of the aspects of the rite that ought to be looked at, but of course each local community will want to discuss even further the viability of the elements that constitute this ritual complex. What seems most important, in this as in all of our celebrations, is that attention and care be given to each of the elements that goes into the entire ritual.

GENERAL INTERCESSIONS

Idle musings in one's spare moments can produce some interesting scenarios. One recent reverie envisioned an "exit poll" of every adult Catholic who worshiped in the United States on a given Sunday. One simple question was asked: "Can you tell me what you prayed for today during the general intercessions?" The results of this carefully scientific data-gathering process can now be released: 2% of the respondents were able to give some idea of three or more intentions; 15% remembered two intentions (usually, "the sick" and "the dead"); 20% could only squeeze out a single idea; 20% confessed to complete short-term memory loss; and 38% didn't know what the general intercessions were!

The point of this fantasy, of course, is that a potentially very significant segment of our Sunday worship experience stands in dire need of attention. The restoration of the general intercessions was one of the jewels of the liturgical reform of Vatican II; but in all too many parishes today, it is a gem that still remains to be polished. What follows are some ideas that may help to make the intercessions an important moment of prayer for our worshiping assemblies.

UNDERSTAND THE PRAYER

It is surprising how often one still hears examples of general intercessions that reveal a lack of understanding of the nature, structure, and form of this prayer. The *General Introduction to the Roman Missal* and the sample intercessions listed in the sacramentary give a concise view of what sort of prayer this should be; in addition, the Bishops' Committee on the Liturgy has issued an excellent background paper that gives a clear and simple introduction to the prayer. Whoever is involved in the development of the weekly intercessions needs to be well versed in this basic information.

Briefly, we need to underline that the structure of the general intercessions involves a presider's address to the assembly to pray, followed by the intercessions with the people's response, a closing prayer to God by the presider, and the people's Amen. The intercessions themselves should be petitionary prayer, not words of praise or thanksgiving. And the scope is meant to be general in nature, as reflected by the four suggested categories of petition that ought always to be included (church, world, needy, and local).

Experience has shown that there are several pitfalls that need to be avoided in composing the petitions. Routine, while it has an important place in ritual prayer, can also deaden. The intercessions, if allowed to become merely routine, will fail to register in any significant way. Covert didacticism, sermonizing. and adversary bashing are all mortal sins when it comes to writing the intercessions. Trivialization and narcissistic self-absorption are also vices that can lead to grave sin and should be avoided at all costs. Finally, one must walk the delicate balance between prayers that seem to suggest that God will do it all for us, and so focusing on our efforts that the God of grace and mystery is lost. The best prayers are those that focus on God, but also empower and energize us to build the kingdom in the ways and areas for which we pray.

DECIDE THAT THIS PRAYER IS IMPORTANT

We tend to devote our energies to what we consider important. Perhaps the malaise regarding general intercessions in so many parishes reflects a failure to decide that these really are important prayer. Once that decision is consciously made, energies will be directed in ways that will surely enhance the prayer. But a commitment is necessary – a commitment of time, attention, resources, and so forth.

What is being suggested here is the need for a kind of conversion regarding the significance of this element in the Sunday worship experience. What is necessary is a genuine conviction that when we pray the general intercessions, what is at stake is the life of the world! It is for the life of the world that the Christian community gathers to pray. And our belief is that we utter before the Father human words that name the pleadings of the Son in the power of the Spirit. Our prayer, our words – we are convinced – represent the unfolding of God's salvific plan whose price was Calvary and whose mandate is the missionary charge for which we have been baptized into the Paschal mystery. These prayers are words of power, words that are meant to galvanize our own concerns for the building of the kingdom as well as God's gracious care on our behalf.

CALL FORTH THE GIFTED ONES

One way to produce the necessary intentions each week is for an already overextended staff person (liturgist, presider, or whomever) to squeeze in a few hurried minutes at the typewriter late Friday or Saturday, trying as best as possible to remember just what the "specials" are this week that need to be included (second collection for left-handed pipefitters, blessing of dogs and dolls at the 9:30 Mass in the gym, archbishop's request for prayers for the fundraiser for a clergy retirement home). Or, a more thoughtful way might be given a chance.

Like every other important ministerial need, the community needs to discern who are the gifted ones placed by the Lord to serve in the specialized capacity required for the parish prayer. Someone who is thoughtful and organized is needed to keep track of those regular and exceptional "special occasions" in the life of the local and wider community. These are the items that somehow often get forgotten until someone outside of church asks, "Why didn't we pray for . . . ." There is also need for someone who has that special gift of sensitivity, of empathy, for those whose hurt cries are often muffled or lost in the whirl of our hectic routines. We need someone who remembers the little ones, who reads the daily newspaper and connects with the suffering behind the headlines, and reminds us that it is our duty to pray for such folk. There is also need for someone who is theologically astute – not necessarily schooled and credentialed, but surely aware of how to say things in religious language that does not embarrass or slip into heresy. There is also need for a wordsmith who has a flair for poetry. Not the poetry of Hopkins; rather, someone more in the tradition of Frost or Sandburg, who can capture in simple, clear language images that touch heart as well as heads. Finally, there is need for the ordinary folk of the parish to have a say in what must be brought to them in prayer. Some mechanism – a book in the vestibule or a more deliberate outreach to ask them what concern tugs at their hearts enough to make them really want to pray over it – some mechanism must be found to give voice to the church that gathers every Sunday in the last four pews. For example, a blank-paged book might be placed on a lectern in the vestibule for people to write their own petitions. It could be left there for all to read, or it could be brought into the liturgy in some appropriate way.

A few lucky parishes will be able to find one or two individuals who will regularly turn out lists of intercessions that move not only God but a sleepy or bored congregation as well. But most of us will have to go to the extra effort of creating structures that gather a variety of persons, so that their diverse, partial gifts can be brought together to produce general intercessions that live up to the potential envisioned by the liturgical reform. My guess is that most parishes could find a group of three to five persons who would be willing to meet for forty-five minutes on Saturday after the morning Mass to do "the people's work" (=liturgy) for the common good. Working from suggestions provided by the parish staff, the group should be able to brainstorm, discuss, and pray over their own ideas and then craft petitions that come from the deeper recesses of the heart.

PRAY THE PRAYER WELL

The final note that must be added has to do with how the general intercessions are actually prayed in the Sunday assembly. If all that is suggested above has been observed, the power of the prayer could still be easily lost if it continues to be mumbled by a rushed lector anxious to move briskly from creed to offertory. The intercessions are important in their own right, and so must they be prayed. Liturgical directives suggest the deacon as the ideal one to name the petitions for the community, but also permit a cantor or another person to exercise that role as well. Nowhere is it suggested that the lector is the appropriate person to read the general intercessions.

The manner of praying the intercessions should be carefully thought through and planned so as to allow the importance of the moment to stand out. In this prayer, the people of God exercise the priestly function assigned them at baptism, by which they are to pray for the life of the world. The pace should be unhurried, with ample silence to allow all to enter deeply into the heart of the prayer. If a decision is made to have the intentions sung, that more solemn form must be done well enough to enhance the prayer, and not merely be change for variety's sake. When all is said and done, a sure criterion for evaluating if a community has prayed the intercessions well is whether or not they are left with a feeling that they have just done something very, very important. If that feeling is not palpably present, then something is amiss. On the other hand, when it is present, then everyone in the assembly will know for certain that they have just prayed in spirit and in truth. At that point, the purpose of the general intercessions will have been accomplished.

PREPARATION OF THE GIFTS (PART I)

A friend of mine recently said, "I think the offertory is the most abused rite we have." At first I disagreed, but on more careful reflection, I began to think he might be correct. When I remember some of the grade school Masses I have attended, where everything from bats and balls to books and bicycles was presented in solemn liturgical procession; when I remember how often posturing ushers have stolen the show with their ingenious ways of gathering money; when I calculate how many person-hours have been spent by folks waiting impatiently while organizers of the procession fumble around in the vestibule to find bread or gift bearers . . . well, my friend may just be right!

Here we look at this important transitional rite in the eucharistic liturgy and try to come to a better sense of what is recommended and what is not. We will concentrate on the objects that are involved, the gifts themselves, and in the next article on the ritual choreography of their preparation.

What are "the gifts" we offer at the Eucharist? The question is deceptively simple, because an accurate answer has many levels of response. To be clear, it is important to start with first things first: The fundamental "gift" which we offer at every Eucharist is the one that we in turn have been given: Jesus Christ in his obedience to Abba, expressed in the Paschal mystery of his life, death, and resurrection, a self-sacrificial offering to God that has accomplished once and for all the salvation of the world. Ultimately, this is the one and only gift we have to offer to God. In the words of the eucharistic prayer: "We bring you the gift you have given us: the sacrifice of reconciliation."

SACRAMENTAL SYMBOLISM

Our offering of that gift, however, is always accomplished by means of sacramental symbols. It is through the symbols of our sacraments that we are able to express the link of our own lives with the gift that is Jesus Christ. This is the reason it is so important that we attend carefully to the issue of sacramental symbolism, here, as in all aspects of our liturgical celebrations.

The American bishops' document, *Environment and Art in Catholic Worship*, contains many important insights into these issues, but regarding the symbols of bread and wine in particular it says: "A second common problem in the use of symbolic objects is a tendency to 'make up' for weak primary symbols by secondary ones. It is not uncommon, for example, to make extensive and expensive efforts to enrich and enliven a Sunday eucharistic celebration without paying any attention to the bread that is used or to the sharing of the cup. *Bread and wine are primary eucharistic symbols* (emphasis added) yet peripheral elements frequently get more attention" (EACW, #87).

Bread broken and offered, wine poured out and shared, these are the primary symbols of the "gift" that we offer. These symbols are not arbitrary; they are what Jesus himself chose to use at the covenant meal of the new dispensation, and it was his words that linked their meaning inextricably to his act of obedient self-sacrifice.

STRONG PRIMARY SYMBOLS

In this light it becomes easier to see why liturgists insist on the importance of bread that looks, smells, feels, and tastes like bread, and wine that is shared with all who approach the table. The primary eucharistic symbols of bread and wine, if they are weak, cannot help but reflect negatively on the celebration as a whole. We recall another fundamental liturgical principle articulated by the American bishops: "Good celebrations foster and nourish faith. Poor celebrations weaken and destroy it" (*Music in Catholic Worship*, 6). Any parish that is still carrying forward wafers that look like plastic and a tiny cruet of wine must do some serious soul-searching as to how they can defend such liturgical minimalism with regard to primary eucharistic symbols.

SECONDARY SYMBOLS

Once a community has made certain that it is highlighting appropriately its most important sacramental gifts, it must look at how it is dealing with the secondary symbols that are part of Catholic tradition. Here, we refer to the "money and other gifts for the poor or for the church" that are collected or brought forward at this time (GIRM, #49). Secondary does not mean unimportant, and so here too a community needs to reflect carefully on how these symbols are handled.

"Money and other gifts for the poor or for the church": How is it that our tradition has identified these and suggested their connection with the primary symbols of bread and wine? The answer, it seems, has to do with what we referred to above as our "fundamental gift," namely, Jesus Christ in his obedient self-sacrifice. At the Eucharist we are linked to the sacrifice of Jesus Christ, not just by engaging in certain symbolic rituals. Our deepest linkage is achieved when we are able to join our hearts and minds to Christ's in a single attitude of obedient surrender to God's will. Our "gift" of the obedient Christ at Eucharist is authenticated when we join to it our own personal gift of self with similar interior dispositions.

The offering of money or gifts for the poor and the church is one highly personal way that we can enflesh such an interior attitude. The self-giving that is embodied in our donation of those material goods is meant to conform us – body and soul – to the meaning of the symbolic gifts of bread and wine that we also offer. We are joined to Jesus' caring for the poor by our gifts for the poor; we are joined to Jesus' efforts to proclaim and build God's reign by our support for the church.

It is important not to leave too implicit the fact that money collected in the baskets goes to the poor as well as to the local parish. More and more parishes that ask their members to tithe are announcing at the collection each week which segment of God's "poor" will receive ten percent of the offertory revenues. Similarly, many communities are also gathering actual gifts of food and clothing for the poor each week, in addition to money offerings. These are excellent practices, as long as they are not allowed to crowd out the primary symbols of bread and wine.

OTHER SYMBOLIC GIFTS

What of the earlier lament of school Masses with bats and balls, books and bicycles? Are they to be totally forbidden? The answer to that question will have to be made at the local level in every case, but in light of the above, several criteria will first have to be addressed before these third-order symbols can be properly used.

First, have the primary symbols received proper treatment? Next, have our traditional "secondary" symbols their proper place? Will using yet another set of symbols crowd out or distract from what must remain primary and secondary? Finally, do those other symbolic elements fit with the sense of "gift" we described? What is their link with the self-sacrifice of Jesus and how clearly is it expressed? (Remember the basic rule: if the symbol requires lengthy explanation to be understood, it probably does not belong.) Does bringing forward these particular objects make sense? Does it powerfully evoke the worshipers' share in the Paschal mystery of Jesus?

I would venture that most bats and balls, books and bicycles do not. However, after thoughtful catechesis, a group of youngsters might be able to find symbols to express the way they have spent some of their summertime caring for others and giving of themselves. Likewise, at a wedding it is possible that a couple may be able to avoid sentimental expressions of their romantic preoccupations and find some suitable way to express their commitment to lead a life for others. But what is too often found in such situations is a collection of implements of work or play, artifacts of a beloved deceased, or objects of hope or promise that really have little to do with the fundamental symbolism of the "gifts" as we have been discussing them here.

PREPARATION OF THE GIFTS (PART II)

Above, we discussed the gifts that are involved in the preparation rite. Here, we discuss the ritual choreography in which those gifts are gathered, presented, and prepared.

THE GATHERING

Since we are dealing here with a ritual action, the way in which gifts are collected is an issue of considerable significance. In many, if not most, parishes, the time spent on this simple task is excessive and disproportionate to its relative liturgical "weight." In a church with twenty rows of pews, why have two ushers stop at twenty rows each, when four ushers could handle ten rows in half the time? Similarly, why pass only two or four baskets hand-to-hand, when twelve or twenty would accomplish the same task more quickly and efficiently? Don't misunderstand. The goal is not speed; every appearance of haste is to be avoided. The goal, rather, is to gather the gifts with dignity and without needless delay.

An obvious, but often overlooked, issue is the need for ushers to be prepared to start their task as soon as it is time. There is little symbolic value to the waiting that occurs while ushers fumble to find the baskets. Once the general intercessions have been completed and everyone is seated quietly, the presider may wish to remind the assembly in a few brief words that their sacrificial offering links them to the sacrifice of Christ and will be used for the poor as well as for the spread of God's reign. Parishes that tithe a portion of their contributed income may wish to remind everyone at this point how their offering will be used.

That done, the ushers should begin to gather the gifts while the ministers prepare the table by setting out the corporal, purificator, chalice, and missal.

Where it is the custom to gather actual gifts of food or clothing for the poor, this is usually best accomplished by having large baskets at the entrance to the worship space as people arrive, and then bringing the baskets forward once the money offerings have been gathered. Otherwise, the logistics can be awkward.

Some communities invite the children to come from their seats at this time and place the foodstuffs in containers before the altar. While the sight of children is always endearing, this practice discriminates against the adults who are present without children. It also gives the false impression that making such an offering is "kid's stuff," something we outgrow when money is regularly in our pockets. Of course, on an occasional basis, a community may ask all those who have brought gifts of food to bring them forward themselves and place them before the altar. On Thanksgiving, for example, this can offer striking witness to the meaning of the feast. On a regular basis, however, such a practice could overburden the rite and give it undue attention.

THE PRESENTATION

After the gifts are gathered, the next gesture in the choreography of this ritual action is their presentation. It is important to recall that the liturgical genre of this segment of the ritual is the procession. Our Roman tradition makes much of pro-

cessions, and the symbolic dimensions of this stylized movement should not be lost on the assembly. It is the people of
God on pilgrimage who make this presentation to the
presider, representatives of the gathered assembly who "go
up to the altar of God" in order that the church's sacred meal
may be prepared and celebrated.

The level of formality with which the procession is
organized should be varied to suit the occasion. The principle
of progressive solemnity would suggest that careful thought
needs to be given to the choices here. The aesthetics of altar
servers scurrying down the aisle with cross and candle, only
to make a U-turn to lead the procession, certainly leaves much
to be desired. Who actually carries the gifts is also an element
that requires due consideration. The ancient reference to those
who "present their gifts at the altar" was an expression used
to describe those who were admitted to share Communion.
Knowledge of these ancient roots raises questions about the
suitability of toddlers or non-Catholic spouses being handed
the bread or wine for the procession. It is also important, in
choosing who will be in the procession, to reflect the diversity
of the entire assembly and not just pick the same few parishioners week after week out of routine. Jesus made a point of
inviting to table those who were judged unsuitable by his
pious contemporaries. In some of our parishes today, in order
to be chosen to carry forward the gifts, one must have clean
fingernails, "proper" dress, and 2.5 children. Better to follow
the lead of the Master and choose for the procession those
who nowhere else in their lives have an experience of being
specially "chosen."

PREPARATION PRAYERS

Once the gifts have been gathered and presented, the presider
prepares them with several prayers. In the original proposal
for the reformed order of the Mass, there was virtually nothing left of the old "offertory prayers" at this point. It was

recognized that the action of preparation had, over the centuries, become redundant, doubling the central offering, which is the eucharistic prayer. The original proposal to do away with the prayers completely was too radical for many, however, and a compromise was struck that left us with the present preparation rite. Unfortunately, the text of the blessing prayers said while the presider slightly elevates the bread and wine are very attractive, and many presiders are loathe to say them silently as the rubrics suggest. It would be much more in the spirit of the reformed liturgy, however, to avoid the double offering, at least for the congregation, by reciting the prayers silently while suitable music is played. In fact, all of the presider's prayers and actions (raising of the elements, hand washing, etc.) should be done with minimal display. After the heavy dose of verbiage during the liturgy of the word, most assemblies need some "quiet time" to rest and prepare themselves to absorb the important words which follow in the liturgy of the Eucharist. All that the presider is doing is preparing the table at this point, and a good host rarely calls attention to himself while setting the table! The fact that many still refer to this section as the "offertory" instead of the "preparation of the gifts" is proof that we have not yet succeeded in the aim of the reform.

A final word must be added about the relative importance of the preparation of the gifts within the entire eucharistic liturgy. While our remarks have emphasized the importance of a careful and thoughtful approach to every aspect of the rite, one must not lose sight of the fact that it is meant to be a minor, transitional ritual between the major actions of the liturgy of the word and the liturgy of the Eucharist. "Little things mean a lot" here, as elsewhere. Yet we should keep those 'little things' in proper perspective. Less is more, and it seems that the ideal is to move quietly and smoothly through this section of the eucharistic rite so that the assembly will be fresh and attentive as the presider announces the eucharistic prayer.

THE EUCHARISTIC PRAYER

A growing number of parishes without resident pastors are becoming accustomed to Sunday liturgical celebrations in the absence of a priest, even preferring them to Masses presided over by a visiting priest with little or no ongoing connection to the community.

Disturbed that such "alternative celebrations" may become long-term, some Catholics blame the church's stand against a married priesthood for the clergy shortage that gave rise to it. Some theologians have begun to write about the "right" of the baptized to Sunday Eucharist, arguing a variety of positions that includes the possible validity of Eucharist presided over by the nonordained.

Meanwhile, parishes that do celebrate Sunday Eucharist must ask themselves this crucial question: How can our parish foster a better celebration of (hence, appreciation for) the eucharistic prayer?

The answer involves both catechetics and liturgy. Thus, a long-range, overall parish strategy to develop better understanding of and participation in the eucharistic prayer by every age group is a valuable first step, which would involve coordinating those responsible for the religious formation of children, youth, and adults. Liturgy committees will also play a vital role in preparing weekly and seasonal celebrations.

Catholics need to understand:

- how the eucharistic prayer fits into the overall structure of the Mass;
- what the chief elements of the eucharistic prayer are (see the GIRM, #55);

- which basic attitudes and skills enable the believer to enter fully into the prayer.

The liturgical celebrations themselves have a pedagogical dimension, as pointed out in *The Constitution on the Sacred Liturgy*. The need to improve the way the eucharistic prayer is celebrated, then, cannot be overstated. The assembly must experience the prayer as a powerful, integral proclamation of what is central to the Christian faith.

POSTURE

Currently, several practices seem to work against such a parish goal. The first is the matter of posture. If asked when the eucharistic prayer begins, most Catholics would say that it begins after the singing of the "holy," when everyone kneels down. (The decision of the American bishops to direct the assembly to kneel at that point may have done more to impede a healthy understanding of the eucharistic prayer than any other single action they have taken.) Few people experience the opening of the preface dialogue as the beginning of the eucharistic prayer because our body language gives no such signal. It is virtually impossible to kneel *after* beginning the prayer without feeling that a break has occurred.

Furthermore, the passivity suggested by kneeling posture isolates the presider, who alone stands (which is the most ancient and traditional prayer posture), from the assembly, which looks on as "observers." The separation of presider from assembly reinforces a "spectator mentality," which runs counter to "full and active participation" that is to be "the aim above all else" in our efforts at liturgical renewal (CSL, #14). Until we all can stand together for the entire proclamation of an unbroken eucharistic prayer, confusion will reign in the popular mind about when the prayer actually begins.

SUNG PRAYER

A renewed celebration of the Eucharist also calls us to respect its nature as a sung prayer. The revision of the sacramentary currently underway will print in first place a simple chant version of each eucharistic prayer, suggesting that the sung form is the customary manner of proclamation. But there is no need to wait for its publication. Liturgical composers have already begun to provide music that integrates both the presider's and the assembly's song into a single musical framework. Although some of the music is still of questionable quality, and some requires musical ability beyond the reach of most presiders, we have made a start in the right direction. I hope suitable music will continue to be published, combining the presider's text and the assembly's three sung acclamations in a single composition.

Even without new music, parishes can exercise creativity in devising ways to help everyone experience the unified nature of the entire prayer. For example, starting with the preface dialogue and continuing through to the final amen, the prayer could be accompanied softly (by a lute, guitar, piano, organ), providing a single musical fabric that links all of the sections of the prayer. If the presider is completely nonmusical, a cantor might "echo" in song key phrases of the prayer after they are spoken by the presider, which the assembly could repeat after the cantor in responsorial fashion. Such an arrangement could heighten the assembly's sense of involvement in praying the prayer, without compromising the liturgical principle that it is the presider who leads the eucharistic prayer of the community. Adaptations ought to allow the assembly to experience the unity of the entire prayer, while offering at the same time their full and active participation in it.

DISTRACTIONS

Several other customs worth mentioning tend to work against the integrity and inclusivity of the eucharistic prayer.

The ringing of bells at certain points is disruptive and reinforces a "magic moment" mentality among the faithful.

Brightening the light focused on the altar during the eucharistic prayer while dimming the area of the assembly also tends to make spectators rather than participants out of the assembly, while isolating the priest.

Peripheral activity in the worship space, such as ushers taking up the collection or children returning from their own liturgy of the word, should be completely finished before the eucharistic prayer begins. While I deeply revere the many contributions the Knights of Columbus have made to the church, I must also say that the custom of an "honor guard" coming forth (even without drawn swords!) seems out of keeping with the aims of a renewed celebration of the eucharistic prayer. A similar critique applies to processions or special shows of paraphernalia by servers, masters of cere-mony, or others, which tend to disrupt the flow of the prayer or distract from its proclamation. In some instances even concelebrants stepping in to say certain parts of the prayer have the undesired effect of disrupting rather than enhancing the proclamation.

THE LITURGY COMMITTEE

A parish liturgy committee desiring to assess the way the eucharistic prayer is celebrated would be well advised to embark first on a study of the theology and structure of the prayer itself, before pushing forward with "improvements." The presider(s) might also be invited to take an active role in the reflection/study process, since an exchange about im-proving both the presider's and congregation's roles is at issue.

Presiders run the risk of falling into bad habits simply because they repeat the prayer so often. Most would deeply appreciate trusted friends who would work with them to improve the pacing and expression of their proclamation. Presiders cannot see their own body language, so it is important for the committee to reflect with them on it as well. The ritual gestures and posture of the presider are crucial to an effective proclamation of the prayer. Some presiders fall into lazy habits in their selection of which prayer to proclaim. Which prayer – of the nine approved – is most appropriate at a given celebration ought to be a matter of prayerful consideration by the committee.

The committee should also consider environmental and artistic issues. Has the altar become cluttered with candles, flowers, or other items so that the focus on bread and wine is lost? Are the elements visible – with fresh-baked bread in a single container and wine in a single decanter with a single cup?

It is impossible to overstate the importance of the eucharistic prayer in our liturgical tradition. Yet, the presider's effective proclamation of it, and the assembly's understanding and active participation in it have received too little parish attention. I hope the points offered here help the parish liturgy committee seeking to consider carefully how it might improve the celebration of the eucharistic prayer in its own community.

VII.

LEAVING GRACEFULLY

The topics I have written about in the *Church* column over the last ten years have included nearly every aspect of the Sunday Eucharistic ritual. One segment of the rite I have never touched upon, however, is the conclusion of the Sunday celebration. Perhaps this neglect is symptomatic of a pervasive pattern among pastors and parish liturgy teams. By and large, we simply don't give much time or attention to how we conclude our Sunday Eucharist. The following remarks may help remedy such habitual indifference.

SIGNIFICANT DEPARTURES

The concluding rite occupies a relatively minor position in the overall complex of ritual words and actions that constitute the Sunday Eucharist. The *General Instruction of the Roman Missal* includes this brief description: "The concluding rite consists of: a) the priest's greeting and blessing which is on certain days and occasions expanded by the prayer over the people or other solemn form; b) the dismissal which sends each member of the congregation to do good works, praising and blessing the Lord." (GIRM, #57) In the Order of Mass itself, there is an expanded vision of this segment, which mentions optional announcements and three forms of the blessing: a) the simple form; b) the solemn blessing, c) the prayer over the people; this is followed by three forms of the words of dismissal and the rubrical choreography of kissing the altar and a reverenced departure.

Pastoral reflection on these elements suggests that their diminutive status in the overall Eucharistic ritual belies their real importance. How people assemble and how they depart are both crucial elements governing the character of any social gathering. Few parishes are exempt from the exodus of worshipers that takes place *before* the concluding rite, as the Communion ritual is beginning and is still in progress.

Theologians, liturgists, and pastors may prefer to deny the implications of such a widespread phenomenon, but social scientists would insist that it bears careful consideration if we are to understand what has transpired throughout the entire worship event. We intuitively recognize the distinctive character of communities where the Eucharistic ritual concludes with the enthusiastic participation of the whole assembly, followed by a period of extended socializing before the congregants depart.

Imagine our reaction if large numbers of concert-goers got up and left during the last movement of a symphony, or if a theater started emptying ten minutes before the curtain was lowered on the last act. Critics would write that the audience had panned the event with their feet and that the performers or cast had better improve quickly if they hope to survive. It is a bit different in the sports arena, where we are not surprised to see crowds thin out early when the outcome of the game is already decided (especially when their team is losing). But when the game is a cliff-hanger, early departures would be surprising.

Why is it, then, that we accept as routine the early departure of worshipers from Sunday Eucharist? Wouldn't we be scandalized if those same congregants prematurely bolted for the door at a funeral or wedding?

These considerations suggest that the concluding rite at Sunday Eucharist is of more than minimal importance and merits the attention of liturgy teams concerned about the overall effectiveness of the community's worship. I have long been convinced that nowhere is an individual's (or a parish's) implicit ecclesiology more evident than in how he or she behaves in the concluding rites. Quite simply, the person who always heads for the door as soon as Communion begins believes something very different about the nature of church and sacrament than does the person who regularly remains after the ritual has ended in order to connect with other parish members and "build up" the community by a ministry of presence. In a variety of subtle (and sometimes not so subtle) ways, parish leaders inevitably signal to the community at large a set of expectations regarding such issues that influence the community's value system and self-understanding.

ANNOUNCEMENTS

Many parishes, for example, make announcements right at the beginning of the concluding rite. By contrast, parishes that continue the pre-Vatican II custom of making announcements at the time of the homily have probably capitulated to a hopeless attitude that extracts worshipers to leave Mass early. Generations had been taught that being present for the "offertory, consecration, and Communion" fulfilled the Sunday Mass obligation, and so they developed the habit of leaving as soon as their obligation was fulfilled. Why stay a minute longer? On the other hand, parishes that see the shared life of the community as integral to the formation of a worshiping assembly are more likely to take some time for announcements that build up the community.

A great deal can be learned about a parish by listening to its announcements: Are announcements reserved exclusively to the pastor, a time for him to scold, cajole, and put forth his personal agenda? Or are they a time when various parishioners emerge as leaders, addressing the assembly on important community issues? Are the announcements mostly about money? service to the larger community? internal housekeeping matters?

Parish liturgy teams would be well advised to reflect on how the announcement time is being used, who composes the announcements, who voices them, and so forth. Some parishes where leadership is widely shared have developed the custom of asking for announcements not from the pulpit/presider, but simply from whoever in the assembly signals that they have something to say to the entire community.

FINAL BLESSING

The sacramentary provides three forms for the final blessing, together with numerous textual options for the solemn blessing (Form B) and the prayer over the people (Form C). However, there is no indication as to the criteria to be used in deciding whether and what alternative blessing to use if the simple forth (Form A) is *not* chosen. Many solemn blessings are connected to particular feasts or seasons, but several others are more "ordinary" in nature. The prayers over the people contain a wide range of intercessory motifs that require some study to sort out just what is most appropriate for a given Sunday. In practice, however, decisions about using this material often appear to be made on the spur of the moment by the presider, when a more thoughtful approach would be better. Liturgy planning teams may wish to develop an explicit policy offering guidance in this regard. Most presiders would welcome such suggestions.

DISMISSAL

After the words of dismissal comes another set of options requiring thoughtful consideration. In many parishes, a closing or recessional hymn accompanied by exit procession is *de rigueur*, and alternatives are not entertained. But, in fact, the sacramentary never mentions resorting to music at this point, though it does seem that some sort of musical accompaniment is called for as a way of concluding the ritual action. Those who prepare the liturgy should decide whether the music is to be an instrumental, a choral performance piece, or a communal song. This is often the time liturgical ministers reassemble for the recessional, but it may be judged better on occasion for the presider and other ministers to remain in place during the music. Most of the time, the presider will want to reach the door in time to greet worshipers as they leave. In communities that regularly socialize after the liturgy, the presider may wish simply to stay in place "up front" as the rite concludes to begin socializing within the worship space. Decisions about such choreography serve as powerful cues to the assembly regarding what is expected of them. That is why it is important for the liturgy team to reflect on and discuss what "message" they wish to send.

WHAT'S NEXT?

The pastorally naïve might wish to limit the considerations of the liturgy team to this point. But there is great significance in what transpires as the formal ritual stops. Is hospitality offered and encouraged? Is there a space for gathering that is easily accessible and inviting? Are ushers or other hospitality ministers still "on duty," distributing bulletins and other "take homes," or are worshipers left to scramble for themselves, returning hymnals and picking up hand-outs? What is the "traffic flow" of pedestrians from pew to parking lot? And, what happens in the parking lot once the ritual is over? Are implicit messages given that worshipers should clear the area as soon as possible to get ready for the next Mass? Is talking encouraged in the worship space? Or is it clear that silence is to be maintained until one exits the room? Most of these questions are answered by practice that evolves over time and without deliberate thought. Still, they are enormously formative of the community's attitudes and values.

We Who Are Sent

The sacramentary suggests that the dismissal is meant to send each member "to do good works, praising and blessing the Lord" (GIRM, #57). As an overall criterion by which to judge the effectiveness of the concluding rite, no more telling standard could be set. Surely, there is no single way to accomplish this end. Yet, however a community wishes to arrange its leave-taking it must remain faithful this sense of mission ("*Ite, missa est*"). School of late have begun to look more closely at the ancient "missa" of the Latin liturgy. Some suggest that the origins of our modern sacrament of confirmation may lie in the "ritual sending" that concluded the Sunday Eucharist.

What a wonderful thought: How we conclude our community gathering is connected to the whole theology of anointing with the Spirit and empowerment for mission in the world! Seen in this light, a graceful leave becomes a matter of importance, a matter for every liturgy team to reflect on and address.